Evolution in I

Evolution in Dispute Resolution

From Adjudication to ADR?

Michiel Duchateau, Saskia Fikkers, Lottie Lane and Esther van Schagen (Eds.)

eleven
international publishing

Published, sold and distributed by Eleven International Publishing
P.O. Box 85576
2508 CG The Hague
The Netherlands
Tel.: +31 70 33 070 33
Fax: +31 70 33 070 30
e-mail: sales@budh.nl
www.elevenpub.com

Sold and distributed in USA and Canada
International Specialized Book Services
920 NE 58th Avenue, Suite 300
Portland, OR 97213-3786, USA
Tel.: 1-800-944-6190 (toll-free)
Fax: +1-503-280-8832
orders@isbs.com
www.isbs.com

Eleven International Publishing is an imprint of Boom uitgevers Den Haag.

ISBN 978-94-6236-635-0
ISBN 978-94-6274-449-3 (E-book)

Printed in The Netherlands

PREFACE

This book is the result of the second annual PhD Roundtable Forum of the Netherlands Institute for Law and Governance, hosted by the University of Groningen on the 4th of April, 2014. The Roundtable Forum provided PhD candidates from Dutch universities the opportunity to present their papers in a constructive, mainly 'junior' environment, on the topic: 'Dispute Resolution: a public or private affair?'

We are grateful to all participants of the Roundtable Forum for their valuable contributions. This concerns not only the speakers who have made their work available through the Forum but also the various participants who helped the authors improve their work through lively discussions.

In addition to our gratitude to the authors and participants, we would like to extend our thanks to the scholars who (anonymously) peer reviewed the contributions to this volume. Their valuable comments and insights certainly helped the authors improve their contributions to this volume.

Thirdly, we would like to thank the board of the *Netherlands Institute for Law and Governance* for its financial support and enthusiastic encouragement. Without its support, the Roundtable Forum and this volume would not have been possible.

Finally, we would like to express our gratitude to Hein Scholtens for his help in organising the Roundtable Forum.

It has been a pleasure to organise the Roundtable Forum and edit this volume and we are already looking forward to next year's PhD Forum.

August 2015

Michiel Duchateau
Saskia Fikkers
Lottie Lane
Esther van Schagen

TABLE OF CONTENTS

INTRODUCTION

In the last two decades, the societal context in which the law operates has dramatically been changed by developments such as globalisation and digitalisation. In particular, the combination of the two can lead to complicated legal situations. For instance, many devices enable both consumers and companies to buy and sell goods and services with just a few clicks. However, these transactions often involve multiple parties, such as retailers selling goods, companies hosting platforms on which these goods are sold and credit card companies. Other examples include companies like PayPal providing payment services and multiple transportation companies delivering the goods, each working with its own terms and conditions and several of them being based in different jurisdictions. If a dispute arises over such a transaction, it is not immediately apparent what the best way of settling this dispute is, who should be settling the dispute, and which actors involved have which role to play in settling the dispute.

Similarly, when investors have entered into contracts with states and subsequent complaints about both states' and investors' conduct have arisen, questions on how disputes should be handled, and by whom, have become subject to debate. If foreign investors enter into contracts with host states, they may negotiate for international arbitration rather than traditional adjudication. After all, national judges may exercise deference in evaluating the state's conduct and may be bound by states through national laws that prejudice them against the investors' interests. These are just two examples that illustrate the increased complexity of disputes that public and private actors are asked to settle. Dispute settlement is evolving to cope with challenges like these.

Adjudication through courts is often understood to be one of the most traditional or classical tasks of states. After all, it is an obvious and important aspect of their internal sovereignty. However, non-judicial forms of dispute settlement seem to have become more and more relevant. Rather than opting for traditional adjudication by state courts, parties increasingly seek ways to resolve their disputes in other ways. This development is reflected in state actors' attempts to encourage and regulate alternative forms of dispute resolution (ADR). The use of ADR has progressed differently in relation to different kinds of disputes. The type of dispute settlement that is best suited to a specific type of case heavily depends on factors such as the nature of the parties involved, the nature of the relationship between them, the economic and/or moral value of the dispute, the cross-jurisdictional nature of the dispute, etc. Ultimately, the evolution of dispute settlement has involved the participation of both public and private actors and has taken on many forms. As such, developments have also altered governance structures surrounding dispute resolution. The various contributions in this book will provide further insight into the effect that the drivers for evolution in dispute resolution may have on the governance structure of dispute resolution. For example, if parties seek more expert judgment, or seek to enhance the legitimacy of ADR systems, this may be reflected in the composition of ADR systems or the participation in ADR systems. Further, concerns of legal certainty may be a reason for the publication of ADR decisions, while conversely, a preference for confidential dispute resolution forms an argument against transparency.

In addition, the contributions in this book draw attention to reflections on the governance of ADR and adjudication more generally, which become increasingly relevant as the evolution of dispute resolution continues. For example, questions may arise with regard to the ad hoc structure of some ADR systems, as well as the time needed to settle disputes through adjudication and ADR. This book's examination of the question how to protect the various interests at stake in dispute resolution draws attention to important governance questions that become more urgent as dispute resolution develops further and as more disputes are settled through ADR. For example, with regard to transparency, do parties have sufficient insight in ADR decisions that may bind them? Another important question concerns the composition of tribunals handling disputes – will parties' disputes be handled by expert and independent public or private actors? Especially if ADR systems form an alternative to adjudication, it becomes important to consider the governance of ADR systems. For example, if international investor-state arbitral tribunals are selected as an alternative to traditional adjudication, this book discusses the question whether these tribunals should also exercise deference. However, from a governance perspective, one may also ask whether the governance of these tribunals should meet similar governance standards as those that have developed for adjudication, for example with regard to the training and independence of adjudicators? Are these standards adequately reflected in notions of good governance,[1] and how can they be safeguarded? Which ADR systems are well suited to settle small-scale retail disputes, not only in terms of parties' preferences, but also in terms of accessibility and good governance principles such as transparency, for instance? To what extent should ADR systems leave room for participation of the public, and is participation of the public necessary for legitimacy?

---

1. See further on the concept of good governance Henk Addink, 'Governance and norms: An interdisciplinary approach of good governance', in: Aurelia Colombi Ciacchi et al (eds.), *Law & Governance. Beyond the public-private divide?* Eleven 2013 The Hague, 243.

This book aims to assess the way in which the nature of dispute resolution has evolved, and how the relation between adjudication and different forms of ADR should be understood. Should they be seen as alternative in the sense of interchangeability, or should they be seen as supplementary, suggesting that they add different elements to a broader dispute settlement structure? Dealing with a range of disputes, this book aims to determine the function of different types of dispute resolution in specific contexts, and what can be expected from them. In this sense, it also aims to assess the driving forces for change in several kinds of dispute resolution, whether these are practical considerations or more focused on the protection of particular interests. These questions feed back to the main research question of what the relation between the different types and methods of dispute resolution is and whether they should be seen as interchangeable or as supplementary.

The volume is structured in four chapters, the first being mostly conceptual in nature, while the subsequent three chapters analyse three examples of dispute resolution to demonstrate the different motivations for using a particular form of resolution. The examples chosen are each embedded in radically different governance structures based on different values, showing that there is no general model for 'the' best way of settling disputes. What is the most suitable way of settling disputes highly depends on contextual factors.

The first chapter of this book, by Erlis Themeli, examines how the nature of adjudication as a public good is influenced by competition between jurisdictions. Competition for adjudication is a recent development, particularly in the European Union, where countries try to attract adjudication from foreign litigants. The chapter defines adjudication and views adjudication next to alternative means of dispute resolutions. It addresses the nature of adjudication as a public or private good, and the question of whether this has been altered by the evolution of dispute resolution.

The first part of the chapter focuses on the nature of goods. It explains the non-excludable and non-rivalrous nature of public goods and discusses problems with the production of public goods. In the second part of this chapter, the author distinguishes between the different functions of adjudication: the dispute resolution function, rule creation function and the educational function. Furthermore, court adjudication is positioned between different forms of alternative dispute resolution such as arbitration, mediation and reconciliation. The different functions of court adjudication are further discussed in the analysis of competition for adjudication in the third part of the chapter, where the author examines how competition for adjudication influences the nature of adjudication.

The chapter combines insights of law and economics theory as well as insights from sociology to provide an in-depth description of the nature and function of adjudication in today's society. It illustrates how parties seek alternative ways of resolving their conflicts, which results in adjudication as a marketable good. However, if court adjudication is treated as a private rather than a public good, important functions of adjudication might be in danger. The practice of competition between jurisdictions is therefore a striking example of the evolvement of dispute resolution, since competition has important consequences for certain functions of traditional dispute resolution.

The second chapter, by Safari Kasiyanto, addresses question of whether ADR, in particular mediation, is an efficient alternative to adjudication for resolving disputes arising in advanced payment systems in small-claims retail cases. In examining this issue, the chapter contributes towards answering the main research question of the book as a whole, in terms of using ADR as an alternative, or supplementary means of dispute resolution through traditional adjudication.

The paper uses empirical data to follow recent trends in the ways in which retail payments are made, and the kinds of disputes arising from them. An explanation of traditional dispute resolution and how small-scale retail disputes fits into the system allows the author to compare the efficiency of both traditional adjudication and ADR (in particular mediation) in resolving these disputes. The benefits and limitations of mediation to solve retail disputes are further examined, focusing on how the interests of both parties to the dispute may be best protected. This relates to the book's examination of how to protect the various interests at stake in dispute resolution, and whether different methods should be used in relation to different disputes.

In particular, the chapter's comparison between the efficiency of traditional adjudication and ADR in small-scale retail disputes contributes towards answering the book's primary research question on the interchangeability of adjudication and ADR. In conducting the comparison, the chapter also examines the nature of small-scale retail disputes, examining their characteristics in order to identify the best-suited method for resolving them. Throughout the analysis, the paper considers how to best achieve the accessibility, efficiency and effectiveness of justice in the disputes at hand – one of the central underlying themes of the book.

The third chapter, by Jeanrique Fahner, compares the evaluation of state conduct by traditional courts and investor-state arbitral tribunals, asking whether investor-state arbitral tribunals should exercise similar restraint when evaluating the conduct of states. This chapter highlights the question whether forms of alternative dispute resolution that aim to replace traditional adjudication should adopt similar standards, in particular deference. According to the chapter's argument, however, international investment arbitration does not fulfil a similar function of domestic judicial review, and tribunals need not adopt the restraint visible in national court's rulings on state conduct.

The chapter sets out the arguments for and against deference in international arbitration, and more specifically stresses the function of arbitration from a public law and a private law perspective. The chapter discusses these two paradigms and questions whether international arbitration is a public or a private law regime, and finds that the difference between these two regimes is a normative rather than an empirical one.

In particular, this chapter's comparison between the evaluation of states' conduct in traditional adjudication and in international arbitration addresses the difficulties that may arise if arbitral tribunals exercise a function which is usually reserved for traditional courts. In this setting, the function of courts to evaluate behaviour and settle disputes may be compromised if investors believe that national courts will exercise too much deference, or more drastically, if they do not have sufficient confidence in the independence of courts. However, replacing traditional courts with systems of dispute settlement in accordance with the preference of international investors entails difficulties: how is it possible to ensure that public interests are sufficiently taken into account? The protection of public interests, and the need to respect democratic decisions have led to arguments that international arbitral tribunals should adopt deference, similar to national courts. The chapter takes the perspective that the answer to the question depends on the function of investor-state arbitration. As investor-state arbitration does not fulfil a similar function, and does not take place within the traditional system of separation of powers, the logic of deference should also not apply.

The fourth chapter of this volume, authored by Liuhu Luo, evaluates recent developments in the People's Mediation system of China. As particularly Western readers may not be familiar with this system, the chapter first describes the system and its background. From a comparative perspective, interesting elements include the high level of participation of private actors in this system, and the overarching value of social harmony. Although the Chinese mediation system described is based on the parties' free will to come to an equitable solution of their conflict, Luo shows that its legitimacy is based at least as much on social harmony as on securing rights of individuals.

Next, the chapter analyses the place of the people's mediation system in China's Big Mediation Network and the relation of mediation to 'traditional' adjudication before the courts. It shows that in China, many actors are involved in many methods of dispute settlement at the same time, making it hard to clearly distinguish 'adjudication' from 'alternative dispute settlement'. Although there are clear differences, there is also much overlap between the several systems of dispute settlement.

Luo's contribution of this volume is an analysis that, mostly from a conceptual point of view, describes the added value of the people's mediation system as it is embedded in Chinese society can have besides the court system. Although the mediation system is clearly not meant to replace the court system, with its broad scope of applicability and involvement of both public and private actors, it is an interesting supplement to litigation indeed. The chapter also shows that the values a legal order protects, such as social harmony in this case, can strongly influence the way in which it deals with dispute settlement. In the Chinese case, the balance between social harmony and individual free will is reflected in the combined system of mediation and court adjudication.

Taken together, the contributions of this book make clear that disputes are evolved within vastly different governance structures. However, they do consider similar questions, including: what function does ADR have in relation to traditional adjudication? How does the evolution of forms of dispute resolution affect the legitimacy of both adjudication and ADR? Together, the examples show how the evolution of dispute resolution has been shaped not only by the nature of disputes themselves and the type of parties involved but also by the values that different systems try to protect. Whether a particular form of ADR should be used instead of traditional adjudication will depend upon these values as well as practical considerations.

1 | Sculpturing Adjudication as a Public Good: Competition between Jurisdictions as a Modeling Factor

Competition for Adjudication in Europe and the Dilemma of Adjudication as a Public or Private Good

*Erlis Themeli**

1.1 Introduction

Human society has created many dispute resolution mechanisms. Among them, court adjudication is one of the most recognisable and most used mechanisms. For many, court adjudication and what it entails is a public good. Mainstream scholarship considers goods that are non-rivalrous and non-excludable as public goods. Since adjudication is considered a public good, it comes without saying that court adjudication is considered as non-rivalrous and non-excludable. However, recently court adjudication has been treated and advertised in a different way, apparently being influenced by the competition of civil justice systems. Competition of civil justice systems is a relatively new phenomenon in the EU, where some member states try to "sell" their court adjudication systems as they sell other goods such as their infrastructure and natural resources. If the competition of civil justice systems intensifies, it might affect the way court adjudication as a good is perceived and treated. Starting from here, the purpose of this paper is to explore what can happen in case the competition of civil justice systems intensifies, with a particular focus on the European Union (EU).

As mentioned above, adjudication is considered as a public good and therefore as being non-rivalrous and non-excludable. In case these characteristics are inherent, i.e. attributes which adjudication has without outside interferences, they cannot be changed or it would be extremely difficult to change them. In practice, these are not inherent characteristics of adjudication, but consequences of the stance of the governments towards "public goods". Therefore, in order to change the nature of adjudication as a public good, it is not enough to change the non-rivalrous and non-excludable characteristics, but it is necessary to change the stance of the government. This paper argues that the competition of civil justice systems can influence the stance of the governments and therefore change the nature of adjudication.

To serve the general purpose, the first part of the paper attempts to further define and understand the meaning of *good* and *public good*. Mainstream scholarship has an

---

* PhD Candidate, Erasmus University Rotterdam.

objective approach to public goods, considering all non-rivalrous and non-excludable goods as public goods. To overcome these limits, this paper takes a subjective approach to consider the nature of goods and public goods. This approach is reflected in the definition of public good, which allows for more flexibility to its categorisation and study. Taking this position does not eliminate the non-rivalrous and non-excludable characteristics of public goods, but considers them as acquired rather than inherent characteristics.

The second part of the paper discusses the place of court adjudication in relation to other dispute resolution mechanisms. It is submitted that court adjudication has been privileged by governments by considering it a public good. This privilege has bestowed upon court adjudication its non-rivalrous and non-excludable characteristics. Court adjudication exercises three functions: conflict resolution, law creation and legal education. Not all of these functions have the same features. This division is important because in the competition between civil justice systems, conflict resolution would be the most attractive and most affected part of the court adjudication "package".

The third part of the paper gives a brief description of the competition of civil justice systems in the EU. Countries such as Germany, France and England have been promoting their judicial system as venues for cross-border litigants in the EU. They create the supply side of the competition process, while the demand side is created mostly by companies and lawyers. It is submitted that cross-border litigants are interested only in the dispute resolution part of the court adjudication, and because of this governments consider court adjudication as a private good rather than a public good. It does not mean that court adjudication will cease to be a public good as long as the governments will consider it as such, but its non-rivalrous and non-excludable characteristics will be eroded at the expense of common citizens.

1.2   Goods and Public Goods

In order to answer the research question, it is important to explore the concept of good and public good. The notion of *good*[1] is somehow axiomatic. Many have a notion of its meaning, but no definition is widely accepted. In very broad terms, *good* means everything that brings a utility to someone. This is contrasted by the notion of *bad*[2], which is everything that diminishes utility to someone. In this regard, the person-*good* relationship is subjective and influenced among others by factors such as

---

1. *Good* as a noun and not *good* as an adjective.
2. Some consider *bads* as *negative goods*. See: Foldvary, Fred F., 'Global Public Goods', Encyclopedia of Global Justice (2011) 434, 434.

time, space, emotive situation, wealth, politics and economy. Subjectively, something can be a good for A, but it can be neither a *good* nor a *bad* for B, and furthermore it can be a *bad* for C. Moreover, the relation to *good* is not fixed in time; it might change rapidly. Something that is a *good* now can become a *bad* later.[3] To consider something as *a good*, the personal relation to the *good* at a certain point of time should be taken into account.

In economics, a good is something that brings utility or an economic advantage. Many goods are vested with property rights while legislation is enacted to protect these rights and therefore the economic value of the goods.[4] It goes without saying that societies try to avoid bad, mitigate its effect or transform bad into good and therefore maximise benefits. The same subjective approach, as described above, is needed to assess whether or not something brings an economic advantage and therefore is a good. Moreover, economists distinguish between *goods* and *services*. With this distinction, *goods* are tangibles that bring economic utility, while *services* are intangibles that bring economic utility.[5] Usually, the term good refers to both *good* and *service* unless it is specified that is a *service*.

Goods can be divided in two categories, *public goods*[6] and *private goods*. In this bipolar division, all non-public goods are private goods. Mainstream scholarship defines non-rivalrous and non-excludable goods as pubic goods.[7] Opposite to this, private goods are subject to rivalry and are excludable. By "non-rivalrous" it is meant that

---

3. Two examples: First, the case of aspirin which can be a *good* for a person in a particular medical condition, but it can become a *bad* if the dosage is exceeded; on the other hand, the same aspirin is neither a *good* nor a *bad* to a healthy person. At this point ownership is excluded. In case of ownership, the relation between the aspirin and the person changes again and therefore the person considers the aspirin as a *good*. In this example, aspirin is both *good* and *bad* for the same person but in different conditions. As a second example, consider a rainy day. Farmer A who has his lands uphill which are well drained benefits from rain and considers it a *good*, while farmer B with lands downhill which are not well drained suffers from inundation and considers rain a *bad*; far away, an observer looking the rain and not affected by it considers rain neither a *good* nor a *bad*. In this example, rain at the same time is considered both a *good* and a *bad* by different persons, based on their personal experience with it.
4. Rubin, Paul, 'Public Goods and the Evolution of Altruism: The Case of the Law' (2008) 8 Politics and Life Sciences 26, 28.
5. A perfume is a *good* as it can be touched and used, while a haircut is to be considered a *service* even though the change of hairstyle or length can be touched and felt.
6. Public goods on their own can be divided into *goods, services* and *resources*. Sometimes, these three are called collective goods. See: Foldvary 2011, p. 434.
7. For definition of public good, please see: Van Aaken, Anne, 'Trust, verify, or Incentivize? Effectuating Public Law Regulating Public Goods Through Market Mechanism' (2010) Proceedings of the Annual Meeting (American Society of International Law) 153; Lemieux, Pierre, 'Producing Private Goods Privately' (2012) 35.3 Regulation 8; Rubin 2008, p. 26; Bratspies, Rebecca, 'Global Public Goods: An Introduction' (2010) Proceedings of the 104th Annual Meeting of the American Society of International Law 147; Foldvary 2011, p. 434; Kaul, Inge, 'Global Public Goods', The Princeton Encyclopedia of the World

the consumption of such goods does not diminish the quantity and the quality of the same good for other people. By "non-excludable" it is meant that it is impossible to limit the consumption of such goods and their availability.[8] This approach suggests that non-rivalrous and non-excludable are inherent characteristics of some goods and these goods are called public goods. This definition and categorisation creates some problems because it is difficult to define and agree on the consumption quantity (or quality) needed to meet the criteria of the definition. In some cases, just a small consumption of public goods can lead to scarcity for the rest of the population.[9] Furthermore, in a finite world, it is very difficult to have unlimited resources that can give the possibility to everyone to use them at their will. A simple inventory would indicate that not all public goods have both the characteristics of the definition. Some public goods have only one of the characteristics, for example, non-rivalrous and excludable goods are called *club goods*[10], while rivalrous and non-excludable goods are called *common pool sources*. These kind of goods bear similarities with both private goods and public goods. However, while some of them are public goods others are private goods. If public goods are not strictly related to the non-rivalrous and non-excludable qualities, what is a public good? How could one define it?

As said before, the relation to goods is subjective. As regards public goods, non-rivalrous and non-excludable are not inherent characteristics of public goods, it is the government that decides to "label" something as a public good. Governments consider various goods as public goods, because they play an important role in society. As a consequence, the government obliges everyone within its jurisdiction or related to that government to consider that good a public good. Furthermore, the government tries to endow to this good the non-rivalrous and non-excludable characteristics. Given the non-excludable characteristics of public goods, it is difficult to exclude free-riders. This means that there are always persons who enjoy the utility of public

Economy (2009) 550; Simon Marginson 'Higher Education and public good' <www.cshe.unimelb.edu.au/people/marginson_docs/BERA_London_6September2011.pdf> accessed 26 August 2015.

8.   For some authors, non-excludability is not a necessary element for public goods. See: Foldvary 2011, p. 434.
9.   Tiebout claims that there are many *public goods* which decrease in availability and quality if they are consumed by many other consumers. Examples of this are public schools or highways. He suggests that a *public good* is one which should be produced, but for which there is no feasible method of charging the consumers. This definition is given as a response to the concept of consumption in definitions similar to the mainstream one. See: Tiebout, Charles, 'A Pure Theory of Local Expenditures' (1956) 64/5 Journal of Political Economy 416, 417.
10. For more see: Bodansky, Daniel, 'What's in a Concept? Public Goods, International Law and Legitimacy' (2012) 23 The European Journal of International Law 651; Foldvary 2011, p. 434; Van Aaken 2010, p. 153.

goods, but do not contribute to their costs. Some authors[11] consider national defence, the sun or air as good examples of this.[12] In case someone does not pay taxes, he still enjoys the national defence of that country. This means that he is taking a "free ride". Because of this characteristic, public goods tend to be under produced, and as a consequence, they tend to be financed by governments by coercively collecting taxes.[13] The production of public goods faces two other challenges, market failure and government failure.[14] That is why their production needs collective and cooperative action and, while the costs are concentrated to the producer, the benefits are diffused to many.[15] This is important because court adjudication is considered to be a public good, but as it was shown the label "public good" is in the hands of the governments. Influential factors like the competition of civil justice systems might change the attitude of governments.

As a conclusion, it is submitted that when defining something as a public good the characteristics of the good itself do not play a role. The most important thing is the opinion of the government. If the government considers a good a public good, everyone should follow suit. Non-rivalrous and non-excludable are two desired characteristics that governments try to endow to public goods because of their merits in social, political and economic spheres.[16] One of these public goods is court adjudication. The next section describes the position of court adjudication in relation to other dispute resolution mechanisms and the reason why the government considers court adjudication as a public good.

---

11. Rubin 2008, p. 26; Lemieux 2012, p. 8.
12. Public goods tend to be very abstract. As a concept, it can include general and wide concepts such as: social cohesion, social cooperation, nature, atmosphere, the Moon, knowledge, etc.
13. Lemieux 2012, p. 9.
14. Kaul 2009, p. 552.
15. The production of public goods faces difficulties even when the benefits outweighs the costs. See: Bratspies 2010, p. 147.
16. *Common goods* are another example of goods that are not defined by their characteristics, but by the subjective stance of the government. Common goods refer to everything that benefits all members of a community. For example, when governments save or give incentives to some private companies (private goods), they do it because they consider them so important that they are labelled as common goods. For more see: Moltchanova, Anna, 'Common good', Encyclopedia of Global Justice (2011) 165. An example of goods that are defined strictly as a result of their characteristics are *credence goods*. Credence goods are those that are provided by an expert who also determines the buyer's needs. Buyers of these kinds of goods cannot assess how much of these goods they need, cannot assess how good the good is or even whether or not it exists. Markets of this kind of goods are characterised by fraud and prices not corresponding to costs. For more see: Hadfield, Gillian K., 'The Price of Law: How the Market for Lawyers Distorts the Justice System' (1999-2000) 98 Michigan Law Review 953, 968, which illustrates the concept with the market for lawyers.

1.3   COURT ADJUDICATION AND ITS NATURE

1.3.1   Court Adjudication: Definition and Elements

Court adjudication is a mechanism used to resolve conflicts that otherwise might result in fractures and troubles for individuals and the society. It has been argued that court adjudication's purpose is to find the truth, to bring social harmony or to protect social values.[17]

Different definitions have been used for court adjudication during the last century. The term was initially used in bankruptcy proceedings, to refer to the final declaration of the debtor to be bankrupt.[18] Dexter refers to court adjudication as "the application of general principles to concrete instances by recognised authorities, with the purpose and probable result of determining what shall happen to specified persons, property, or institutions."[19] This definition is important because it is created by a sociologist and therefore departs from the legal stand point. It puts court adjudication in the position of a mechanism created by the society to resolve disputes and not in the position of a legal mechanism. Moreover, a sociological standpoint offers the insights of the social control theory where adjudication plays an important role.[20] This definition contains some elements that are important to the functioning of court adjudication.[21] First, court adjudication functions based on general principles that are applied to specific situations. "General principles" is an umbrella term that includes laws, court decisions or opinions, social norms or other sources of law recognised in a jurisdiction. These principles regulate the general behaviour in society and are recognised and accepted by the parties before the dispute arises. Second, a recognised authority must exist. This authority is represented by the judge and is organised by the state making it universally recognisable. In many cases, conflicting parties do not need to assign or accept the jurisdiction of this authority before the conflict arises. Third, court adjudication determines

---

17. Weckstein, Donald, 'The Purposes of Dispute Resolution: Comparative Concepts of Justice' (1988) 26 American Business Law Journal 605, 606-615.
18. See the voice 'Adjudication' in Henry Campbell Black, 'Law Dictionary: Containing Definitions of the Terms and Phrases of American and English Jurisprudence, Ancient and Modern (West Publishing Co. 1891 St. Paul, MN).
19. Dexter, Lewis A., 'The Sociology of Adjudication: Who Defines Mental Deficiency' (1960) 4 American Behavioral Scientist 13, 13.
20. This is important in view of the discussion in 1.3.2 where the privileged position of the court adjudication in the eyes of the government is discussed.
21. Another definition of court adjudication is "a procedure for determining a dispute involving a claim of legal or customary right in which a third party is invested with the authority to make a decision that is recognized as binding, except that under some systems of adjudication that parties have the right to reach a different disposition by contract after an adjudication".
    For the definition and the elements it contains see: Hazard Jr., Geoffrey C., 'Adjudication as a Private Good: A Comment' (1979) 8 The Journal of Legal Studies 319.

what shall happen to specified persons, property, or institutions. This element is the decision of the court which tries to quell the dispute between the parties.

Some elements of court adjudication are missing from this definition. First, this definition does not provide for any mechanism that would allow the enforcement of court decisions, despite the fact that one of the reasons why court adjudication is used is to give the possibility to use coercive force to enforce the decision. It can be argued that the recognised authority that decides upon the dispute is the same person invested with coercive power to enforce this decision. This is not always true. In countries where power is allocated to different branches, coercive power is applied by the executive branch and not by the judiciary. Court adjudication offers only a binding decision; its enforcement is left in the hands of other authorities. Second, an element that should be added is rationality. The decision-making process is based on a rational consideration of facts and regulations related to the case. Without rationality it would be enough to toss a coin and decide based on the result; after all, the coin is impartial and cheap. Adjudication is not a desultory process and cannot be decided by tossing a coin. It should give the participants the possibility to influence the discussion by presenting proofs and exposing arguments in their favour.[22] This is the third missing element, i.e. the possibility to be represented and to present proofs and arguments. After collecting the elements from above, in this paper court adjudication will have the following meaning: A rational process between two or more parties where a concrete state instance uses logic to apply general principles and regulations; provides the parties with the possibility to be represented and to present proofs and arguments; and decides what shall happen to specific persons, property or institutions in order for coercive power to be used by a competent authority.

Some authors have distinguished the following functions of court adjudication: a dispute resolution function, a rule creating function and a clarification of existing laws (education) function.[23] This set of functions, resulting from a law and economics perspective, are considered not just functions but goods as well. Other perspectives might be different, but still contain the conflict resolution element.[24] It is evident that

---

22. Fuller, Lon L., 'Collective Bargaining and the Arbitrator' (1963) Wisconsin Law Review 3, 19.
23. In this paper, these functions will be used. For more see: Landes, William and Posner, Richard, 'Adjudication as a Private Good' (1979) 8 The Journal of Legal Studies 235, 236; Wagner, Gerhard, 'Dispute Resolution as a Product: Competition between Civil Justice Systems' in Horst Eidenmüller (ed.), 'Regulatory Competition in Contract law and Dispute Resolution' (C.H. Beck, Hart, Nomos 2013 Munich, Oxford, Baden-Baden) 353, 353.
24. A philosophical set of functions for the courts is: ***Resolving specific conflicts*** *between individuals or groups in a manner, which may have some chance of being acceptable even to the loser;* ***serving as a social controller*** *on behalf of the regime;* ***serving as an extension of the administration***, *performing a variety of administrative tasks not involving inter-personal/group conflict.* See: Tate, C. Neal and Haynie, Stacia L., 'Authoritarianism and the Functions of the Courts: A Time Series Analysis of the Philippine Supreme Court 1961-1987' (1993) 37 Law & Society Review 707, 713.

resolving conflicts is the most important function and result of court adjudication. Without this function, court adjudication would not be adjudication. The rule creating function is accepted in common law countries and it is becoming significant for other legal traditions as well. The function of clarifying the existing law has a double purpose: the first is to clarify the law for users; the second is to help the development of legal sciences in general. Clarifying the law helps users to apply the laws better and allows courts and the adjudication system in general to proclaim a certain way of deciding. The knowledge that judges adjudicate in a certain way enables the volume of adjudication to be contained.[25] This happens because parties know in advance how the judge will decide in certain cases and therefore do not go to court for those cases or change their behaviour in such a way that they do not end up in court. This function has a social control effect as well.

1.3.2   Position of Court Adjudication among Other Conflict Resolution Mechanisms: A Privileged Position

This section shows that court adjudication is one of the dispute mechanism that societies have. While this mechanism is important for governments, a society without court adjudication is still possible and functional.

Resolving conflicts is done primarily by fighting or talking. Fighting involves the use of violence to ascertain one's opinion. Fighting and the use of violence challenge the monopoly of power of the (ruling class) government and might become very costly. To restrict fighting and violence, governments apply sanctions to perpetrators of such acts and criminalise their behaviour. Despite restrictions and the criminal character of fighting, there are many instances where fighting is used to resolve conflicts. "Bullies" in schools create and resolve conflicts by using violence or threat of violence. Illicit businesses create conflicts that are resolved by violent acts. So even though fighting is not recognised as a conflict resolution mechanism by the state, it is still present in society.[26]

The other main approach to resolve conflicts is by talking. This implies the use of verbal or written communication and dialogue between rival parties in a conflict.

---

25. For the contribution to science, see: Wagner 2013; Freeman, Michael, 'Lloyd's introduction to Jurisprudence' (Sweet & Maxwell 2008 London).
26. According to Weckstein, different types of societies have different objectives as regards conflict resolution. He makes the distinction between societies that put the individual in the center of the conflict and societies that put the welfare of the society in the center of the conflict. The first one tries to understand whether or not the rights of the individual have been violated and takes measures to mitigate them. The second one tries to safeguard the interest of society in general, which is sometime different from the interest of the individual. Modern societies resemble more the first type, while ancient and primitive other resemble the second type. Even in modern societies, there are different groups that resemble the second type of societies and that put the interest of the group before individual interests. They have their own mechanisms of dispute resolution. This section considers only the first type of societies. See: Weckstein 1988, p. 605.

By talking, conflicts are resolved through bilateral consultation between the parties in conflict, or with the intervention of a third party. Bilateral consultation includes conflict resolution methods like negotiation and reconciliation. In case a third party is involved, the dispute resolution process develops into mediation, arbitration or court adjudication (litigation). In the following paragraphs, the different forms of conflict resolution by talking are discussed.

Reconciliation as a dispute resolution mechanism[27] was diffused in ancient and primitive societies. Through reconciliation, parties tried to find a common language to overcome the conflict before it escalated. Reconciliation presupposes the existence of a situation before the conflict (where the parties were in amicable or not so diverging paths) that can be restored. Without this situation and this possibility, reconciliation cannot exist.[28] Going back to the pre-conflict situation was beneficial to the parties and to society because additional costs and further social conflicts were avoided.[29] For the same reasons, reconciliation is appreciated in modern societies.[30] Despite the lack of a universally accepted definition, some elements of reconciliation can be highlighted: unforced willingness of the parties to admit their responsibility and fault to the other party, self-confession, apology and absolution.[31] Reconciliation differs from other conflict resolution mechanisms, as it tries to end animosities between parties and to restore a normal relation between them. In this sense, it is different from other forms of conflict resolution, which are interested in finding a perpetrator for the wrongful act and make that person pay or respond according to the rules.[32]

Negotiation is another form of conflict resolution which does not require the involvement of a third party. Through this process, parties establish a dialogue to overcome the dispute. This dialogue can terminate in four different ways: 1. no agreement; 2. victory for one party; 3. simple compromise; 4. a win-win in which parties achieve a higher joint benefit than would be possible with a compromise agreement.[33] The outcome of a negotiation process would depend on the limits and goals of the parties. If limits and goals are unreasonable, the outcome would be a non-agreement.

---

27. Bar-Tal (2000) considers reconciliation not as a conflict resolution but as an alternative to it. See: Bar-Tal, Daniel, 'From Intractable Conflict through Conflict Resolution to Reconciliation: Psychological Analysis' (2000) 21 Political Psychology 351.
28. Kingsolver, Ann E., 'Everyday Reconciliation' (2013) 115 American Anthropologist 663.
29. Joyner, Christopher C., 'Reconciliation as Conflict Resolution' (2010) 8 New Zealand Journal of Public and International Law 39, 43.
30. The General Assembly of the United Nations proclaimed 2009 as the International Year of Reconciliation. International Year of Reconciliation, 2009 GA Res 61/17, A/RES/61/17 (2007).
31. Joyner 2010, pp. 39, 42.
32. Reconciliation is also called "restorative justice"; while the other forms of conflict resolution are called "retributive justice".
33. Carnavale, Peter J. and Pruitt, Dean G., 'Negotiation and Mediation' (1992) 43 Annual Review of Psychology 531, 535–550.

Mediation is a method of conflict resolution that requires the assistance of a third party to resolve the conflict between two other parties.[34] Scholarship suggests that when parties are in conflict about certain goals but share some others, mediation increases the chances of success in overcoming difficulties.[35] Due to its form, it is used by parties that want to continue their relationship after the resolution of the dispute. During mediation, the dispute and its resolution are treated as private goods which exclude everyone not involved in it.

Another method of resolving conflicts is arbitration. Arbitration is a process where the parties in conflict agree to appoint one or more persons to evaluate upon their claims over a dispute. The decision delivered through this process can be executed and enforced in many jurisdictions. The New York Convention on the Recognition and Enforcement of Foreign Arbitral Awards has been accepted by the majority of UN member states since its adoption in 1959.[36] This shows that arbitration is considered as a reliable and effective source of conflict resolution. Negotiation, mediation and arbitration allow the parties greater control over the procedures and the identity of the decision makers compared to court adjudication.[37] Disputes in arbitration proceedings are considered private goods. Even when one of the parties in the arbitration proceeding is a national government, it is not allowed to disclose details from the proceeding. The public interest in dispute is considered as a *private good* by the government and treated as such in the arbitration proceeding. It could be said that everything that enters arbitration becomes private.

Court adjudication, on the other hand, has been a mechanism of conflict resolution since early in human history. Compared with other conflict resolution mechanisms, court adjudication is not very different. However, court adjudication's characteristics (as defined above) make it appropriate to resolve a great variety of conflicts, including criminal conflicts. People are familiar with it and can recognise it throughout the world. These characteristics made governments recognise the importance of court adjudication and consider it as a public good.[38] The reasons why governments chose court adjudication as their default conflict resolution system can be traced to some circumstances: first, during the evolution of the state, governments wanted to have

---

34. The involvement of a third party might facilitate asymmetric concessions that parties cannot achieve through a bilateral dialogue. In bilateral negotiations, parties make more symmetrical concessions to each other. See: Beardsley, Kyle and Nigel Lo, 'Third-Party Conflict Management and the Willingness to Make Concessions' (2014) 58(2) Journal of Conflict Resolution 363.
35. Weckstein 1988, p. 605; Beardsley and Lo 2014, p. 363.
36. The text of the Convention and some useful links can be found at the website of the United Nations Commission on International Trade Law (UNCITRAL): <www.uncitral.org/uncitral/en/uncitral_texts/arbitration/NYConvention.html> accessed 26 August 2015.
37. Weckstein 1988, p. 605.
38. The definition of court adjudication does not give any clue whether or not it is a public good or a private good.

some reliable conflict resolution mechanism, which they found in court adjudication[39]; second, the elements and functions of court adjudication offer many advantages for governments; third, court adjudication is effective for many types of conflicts, including criminal conflicts.

1.3.3   *Conflicts, from Private Good to Public Goods and Adjudication Provided by Private Parties*

Conflicts revolve around either a public or a private good. The conflict that arises does not follow the nature of the good necessarily. Some conflicts involve a public good, but are considered a private good. For example, many conflicts between governments and private companies involving public goods are resolved by arbitration tribunals.[40] Those conflicts are treated as private goods by the parties interested and the tribunal, even though the character of the *good* is different.[41] Other conflicts involve private goods, but are considered public goods. The reason why these conflicts are public goods is that governments consider them important for the cohesion and tranquillity of the society. In order to filter between the multitude of cases, governments and courts use material and procedural law. If a claim passes the procedural filters and is accepted by the court to be judged, the conflict becomes a public good. Conflicts accepted by the court take the non-rivalrous and non-excludable characteristics of public goods as well. The non-rivalrous character is manifested in the fact that these cases do not have consumption problems. The public can be present at their hearings and attend every phase of dispute resolution. Theoretically, no matter how many cases a court has, it will always deliver the same quality of justice. In other words, the use or disuse of the court will not create problems to consumers. The non-excludable characteristic is manifested in the fact that the outcomes of these cases do not exclude anyone.[42]

After the end of the World War II, many researchers were trying to show that private parties can take over the role of the state in providing services and goods. In 1979, Landes and Posner published a paper where they examined the possibility of private court adjudication from an economic stand point.[43] Their paper starts with the presumption that the court system produces two goods. One is dispute resolution and the other one is rule creation. These two goods can be, and often are, produced

---

39. D'Amico (2010) gives an historical example of how court adjudication for criminal offences went from being private to being public. See: D'Amico, Daniel J., 'The Prison in Economics: Private and Public Incarceration in Ancient Greece' (2010) 145 Public Choice 461.
40. Landes and Posner 1979, pp. 235, 245.
41. Furthermore, the stance of the government towards the good does not change. The good remains a public good, but the conflict is still a private one.
42. The law creation function and the education function are shared with the whole society, while the dispute over the good is solved between the parties in conflict.
43. Landes and Posner 1979, p. 235.

separately. Precedents play an important rule creation role in the Anglo-American legal system, but they are less important in other countries, while dispute resolution is universally accepted as the most important function of the courts system.

In case court adjudication is privatised, public intervention would be necessary in two cases: first, to ensure compliance with the decision of the private judge; and second, to compel submission to adjudication. In this private system, parties would have the right to choose the judge they think is the most appropriate. The rule creation function would face two problems: first, it would be difficult to establish property rights[44] over a precedent and as a consequence judges would have little incentive to produce it; second, precedents of different judges might be inconsistent with each other and thus diminish or destroy their value. For these reasons, Landes and Posner conclude that it would be more likely to see the emergence of a private market for the dispute resolution function than for the rule creation function. This problem would invite the intervention of the public sector in this private market.

In the end, the authors conclude that private courts have limitations for both dispute resolution and rule creation. The authors have an objective view on goods and evaluate them based on their characteristics and not based on the subjective considerations. Critics to Landes and Posner have underlined that they fail to show how a private party would be compelled to submit to adjudication.[45] The authors give some hints on how to resolve this situation, but the assistance of a third party remains the only feasible alternative. This third party would have to review the case, at least as regards the right to submit to adjudication.[46] Two situations can emerge here. First, in case this authority is public, the process of privatisation of the court system would not be finished and the production of dispute resolutions would be, at least partly, a public affair,[47] while the final good will be considered as such by the government. Second, in case this compelling authority would be private,[48] it will suffer from monopoly problems and it might evolve into a public authority.[49]

---

44. Property rights on precedents would allow judges to extract rent from the precedents they created in case they are used by other judges. In a certain way, a precedent can be viewed as a work of art, for which the judge needs its copyrights, and relative royalties.

45. Hazard 1979, p. 319.

46. If this third party does not make such a review, its role would be stained by abuses.

47. Carrington, Paul D., 'Adjudication as a Private Good: A comment' (1979) 8 The Journal of Legal Studies 303, 303.

48. The question as how and who to appoint such third party remains.

49. On the one hand, there is the example given by D'Amico, which describes how adjudication in Ancient Athens developed from privately owned to public owned. See: D'Amico 2010, p. 461.
    On the other hand, Cowen and Friedman discuss the feasibility of an anarcho-capitalist society to build stable private institutions. Cowen concludes that these institutions would evolve into governments. See: Cowen, Tyler, 'Law as a Public Good: The Economics of Anarchy' (1992) 8 Economics and Philosophy 249; Friedman, David, 'Law as a Private Good: A response to Tyler Cowen on the Economics of

Furthermore, Landes and Posner do not have a definition for adjucation. Therefore they fail to recognise the element of "binding" in adjudication.[50] If a private party can decide on a dispute but cannot make this decision binding, then it is not adjudication.[51]

In their paper, the authors claim that the state behaves like a common seller in the market for dispute resolutions and tries to sell as much as possible. In my view the contrary is true; the state tries to make the parties resolve their conflicts away from courts and use courts only as a last resource and only if the conflict is a public good. In a certain way, state courts are interested more in the protection of public interest than in the interest of a particular party.

As regards rule creation, the authors fail to recognise some aspects of it. First, not all the parties to the adjudication are interested in it.[52] For this reason, it is only the state that is interested in creating rules from adjudication and therefore this is always a public good. Another negative aspect of rule creation in the hands of privates is related to democracy. How can a rule created by a private judge for two private parties be applied to the public in general? Is this contrary to the democratic principle of division of power? Should the rule creation be a prerogative of a publicly elected body? These are some of the dilemmas that should be dealt with in case the creation of rules by privates is considered.

As a conclusion, governments decide which conflict should be resolved by the courts. This transforms private conflicts into public conflicts that can be resolved by courts. Furthermore, the majority of the parties are interested in resolving the conflict and only in rare cases in the other functions of court adjudication. If a government would try to privatise court adjudication, they will partially fail since court adjudication will need public presence in furthering its functions.

Anarchy' (1994) 10 Economics and Philosophy 319; Friedman, David, 'The Machinery of Freedom, Guide to a Radical Capitalism' (2nd Edition La Salle, Open Court 1989 IL)

See also: Stringham, Edward, 'Overlapping Jurisdictions, Proprietary Communities, and Competition in the Realm of Law' (2006) 162(3) Journal of Institutional and Theoretical Economics (JITE)/Zeitschrift für diegesamte Staatswissenschaft 516; Caplan, Bryan and Stringham, Edward, 'Privatizing the Adjudication of Disputes' (2008) 9 Theoretical Inquiries in Law 503.

50. Hazard 1979, p. 319.

51. The authors explain organisational aspects of the private court system, but they do not explain how these decisions would be binding. If the arbitration example would be used, it would need the help of a public authority to make the recognition of the decision. Private bailiffs can be used to avoid using a public authority, but private bailiffs might create even larger conflicts with powerful parties that do not accept the decision of the court.

52. Carrington 1979, p. 303.

1.4   COMPETITION FOR ADJUDICATIONS IN THE EU

1.4.1   Competing Countries

In recent years, Germany, France and England have been actively promoting their jurisdictions as venues for adjudication proceedings. The impression is that these countries are competing to attract litigations. So far competition has evolved in a "war of brochures".[53]

In Germany, several associations with the help of the Ministry of Justice have formed an alliance to promote German law and institutions. So far, they published a brochure that explains the benefits of German courts and the efficiency of German law and institutions, with the clear intention to attract parties in their jurisdictions.[54] Similar to the German move, France has created a *Foundation* for the promotion of French law in general and continental law in particular.[55] The aim of the *Foundation* is the promotion of the continental law system *vis-à-vis* the common law system from a purely academic stand point. However, a second aim for the existence of the *Foundation* can be discerned. This second aim has to do with the desire of France and other European continental countries to take part in the British share of the legal market. In England and Wales, the Law Society, with the help of the Ministry of Justice, has been promoting English law as a mechanism for dispute resolution. Part of the ongoing promotion was the publication of a brochure[56] that promoted, among other things, English courts as flexible, efficient and reliable.

These might seem to be indicia rather than proofs for the competition of civil justice systems, but the attention of the government to this process is increasing for some reasons. One of the reasons why these countries compete is because they believe they can make some profit from the fees parties pay to the court. This is not completely true since many courts are subsidised by their governments and therefore are not a source of profit. Another reason for competing can be the revenues that an increased number of cases can bring to the local legal practitioners community. The higher the number of cases the more work for lawyers and other related professions. This is a rather indirect revenue for the government in form of taxes extracted from lawyers, but a better source compared to the direct one. Its importance in the general economic framework is debatable, since the revenues extracted from lawyers might be too small for a

---

53. Vogenauer, Stefan, 'Regulatory Competition through Choice of Contract Law and Choice of Forum in Europe: Theory and Evidence' (2013) European Review of Private Law 13.

54. This initiative is called "Law Made in Germany". For more, see the website: <www.lawmadeingermany.de> accessed 26 August 2015.

55. The Foundation is called *Fondation pour le Droit Continental*. For more, see link to the website of the Foundation: <www.fondation-droitcontinental.org/en/> accessed 26 August 2015.

56. The brochure is titled "England and Wales: The jurisdiction of choice". It was not possible to find the brochure on the website of the Law society. However, the brochure can be downloaded from this website: <www.haitz-rechtsanwaelte.de/de/newsarchiv/data/newsarchiv_56_2.pdf> accessed 26 August 2015.

government to bother with the competition. Nevertheless, in the times of economic distress, no source of revenues can be neglected by the government. In the EU context, it can be argued that competing countries are too big for the competition of civil justice systems to be lucrative to them.[57] But, it is also true that lawyers are a powerful interest group in some of these nations and are pushing these governments to enter the competition "game".[58] In a more strategic and long-term view, governments would be interested in having a competitive court that is attractive to investors and guarantees a good investment climate. In the long-term, this would be beneficial for the government and the economy of that jurisdiction in general. However, the real reasons are not clear and can be very well a combination of all the above-mentioned reasons. All these reasons, combined with the general will of the EU to enhance cross border transactions, free movements of goods and services and the abolition of barriers points at an increasing interest from Member States of the EU at competing with each other in attracting litigants and legal businesses in their jurisdictions.

1.4.2   Aspects of Competition and the Influence to the Nature of Adjudication

The EU is facilitating competition by abolishing barriers and enhancing cross border trade and cooperation. This has increased the number of transactions over the years and therefore the number of conflicts arising from these transactions. To facilitate cross-border conflict resolution, the EU has enforced among others, the Brussels I Regulation[59], which delineates jurisdictional rules in case of cross-border disputes.

These regulations allow parties to choose the court where the conflict will be resolved after it has arisen. Furthermore, parties can use their party autonomy to stipulate in contracts, which court will have jurisdiction over their future disputes. Parties have different criteria to choose a court before and after the conflict has arisen. If a party knows that it will be a plaintiff, that party will choose a jurisdiction that will be favourable to their position. In the case the parties do not know their position in the future, they will be inclined to choose a jurisdiction that is perceived as neutral and impartial

---

57. In the literature about the competition for incorporation, some authors argue that large states do not find competitions for incorporation attractive. This happens because the revenues derived from this competitions are dwarfed by revenues from other sources. In this situation, large states remain inactive and do not participate in competition. On the contrary, for small states the revenues derived from the competition for incorporations are large enough to be lucrative for their budgets. As an example, the revenues derived from attracting firms to incorporate are important in Delaware, but would be negligible for California. For statistics and a theoretical approach to this, see: Bebchuk, Lucian, Alma Cohen and Allen Ferrell, 'Does the Evidence Favor State Competition in Corporate Law?' (2002) 90(6) California Law Review 1775.
58. The cases of the German and British brochures are a typical example.
59. Regulation (EU) No 1215/2012 of the European Parliament and of the Council of 12 December 2012 on jurisdiction and the recognition and enforcement of judgments in civil and commercial matters, OJ L 351, 20.12.2012, pp. 1-32.

to both parties. The exact reasons and their value to the parties is not yet extensively researched.[60] Governments are interested in attracting as many parties as possible, therefore they would try to look as neutral as possible, not to scare away any potential party.[61] Taking into account some of the reasons mentioned in Section 1.4.1, countries would be more attractive if their jurisdiction was perceived as neutral rather than as favouring the defendant or the plaintiff. It should be clear that governments would be more interested to attract companies that could bring more lucrative cases and not individuals who have simple and unprofitable cases. Furthermore, individuals are less mobile and less inclined to choose a court other than the court of their jurisdiction. The Brussels I Regulation regulates exactly this aspect by giving to vulnerable parties, in many cases individuals, the privilege to litigate in their jurisdictions or even be able to choose a jurisdiction that is favourable to them.

In the market for court adjudication, litigant parties form the demand side. Countries, which compete to attract litigations in their courts, form the supply side. The good in this market is court adjudication. In theory, to win a competition race the adjudication mechanism of a state should excel institutionally and legislatively. Institutionally means that courts should be more effective, cheaper and faster than rivals. To show differences between courts, the EU is already assessing the performance of the judicial systems in its Member States.[62] Furthermore, laws and procedures should be attractive for parties by showing impartiality, stability and a good historical record. The competitive race is hampered by the characteristics of legal services as a good,[63] by the psychology of choice-making process[64] and more often by political implications.

---

60. Analysing an empirical research, Durand-Barthez suggests that lawyers are psychologically influenced by the perceived independence of courts, familiarity with the law, and stability of legislation and institutions. See: Durand-Barthez, Pascal, 'The "governing law" Clause: Legal and Economic Consequences of the Choice of Law in International Contracts' (2012) (5) International Business Law Journal – Revue de Droit des Affaires Internationales 505, 510. In another analysis, Vogenauer suggests that indeed familiarity with the systems and perceived sophistication of the system are important factors for the choice of court by the lawyers. See: Vogenauer 2013, pp. 13, 77.
61. Wagner analyses the different type of demand for dispute resolution and different supply in offer. The interaction between supply and demand would create different with different focuses, e.g., favouring the plaintiff or favouring a more neutral approach. In my opinion, neutrality is more important because apart from attracting parties, improves the reputation of the jurisdiction. Wagner 2013.
62. In 2014, the European Commission for the Efficiency of Justice published the 5th edition of the Evaluation of European Judicial Systems. See: <www.coe.int/t/dghl/cooperation/cepej/evaluation/default_en.asp> accessed 26 August 2015.
63. Hadfield 1999-2000, p. 953.
64. As regards psychology of choice making in law, see: Durand-Barthez 2012, p. 505; Low, Gary, 'A Psychology of Choice of Laws' (2013) 24(3) European Business Law Review; Posner, Eric A., 'The Questionable Basis of the Common European Sales Law: The Role of an Optional Instrument in Jurisdictional Competition' (2013) 50(1) Common Market Law Review 261. On the theory of choice in general, see: Salecl, Renata, 'Self in Times of Tyranny of Choice' (2010) 48(50) FKW//Zeitschrift für Geschlechterforschung und visuelle Kultur; Salecl, Renata, 'Society of choice' (2009) 20(1) Differences 157; Schwartz,

As a good in the market, adjudication should be treated by separating its functions of dispute resolution, rule creation and clarification of existing laws (education). As said, all these functions are public goods. It is predicted that the parties in conflict will be interested only in the dispute resolution function. These parties are not interested in rules created by the courts as they follow an immediate interest and do not always have future stakes.[65] The parties are interested even less in the clarification of existing laws (education) function. While the state considers it a public good that increases the utility of the society, private parties involved in the dispute have little interest in it. As a result, the interest of the parties and the market will be directed only at the dispute resolution function of the court.

With the intensification of competition, the nature of adjudication might change as well. Competing states in the EU would offer their court adjudication in the market. They would be receptive to the requests of the market and shape their adjudication system accordingly. It is reasonable to think that competing countries would agree to adjudicate as many disputes as possible and even disputes not strictly related to their jurisdictions. This is also facilitated by Article 25 of the Brussels I Regulation, which allows parties to choose the courts of Member States before the conflict arises. By doing this, states fictitiously consider these disputes as public goods in their own jurisdiction, because they are interested only in the benefits related to attracting litigation and not in the case itself. These disputes do not have any of the desired elements of public goods: they exclude the population of that state because they are not related with that state and the consumption from the disputing parties completely eliminates the population of that jurisdiction. Furthermore, ambitious jurisdictions might offer privacy during adjudication and restrain the public from the courtrooms. While this can be an appealing move for litigating parties, it is a drawback for the public nature of hearings and access to records or publications. Another negative side of this would be the creation of non-transparent precedents with repercussions in the interpretation of law.

The rule creation element of adjudication might be affected by competition as well. So far, rule creation from court decisions in continental Europe is not as important as it is in England. Competition would mean that cases not related or faintly related to the state would be accepted for adjudication as well. Rules that derive from those cases might be difficult to be generalised for the country where the case is being adjudicated for two reasons. First, the applicable law might be that of a different country.[66] Secondly, the interest involved does not relate to the interest of the population in that

Barry, 'The Tyranny of Choice' (2004) 290(4) Scientific American-American Edition 70; Schwartz, Barry, 'Self-determination: The Tyranny of Freedom' (2000) 55(1) American Psychologist 79.

65. Landes and Posner 1979, pp. 235, 260.
66. Rome I Regulation on the law applicable to contractual obligations and Rome II Regulation on the law applicable to non-contractual obligations are the main instruments that designate the applicable law in the EU.

country. For these reasons, the state that organises adjudication might renounce the rule creation function of court decisions. This would look more democratic as it would concentrate law making on the legislative body, but maybe not most suitable move. The problem of non-transparent precedents (mentioned above) will undermine their credibility and value.

The function of clarification of existing laws (education) might get its drawbacks from the competition for adjudication as well. Since disputes attracted by competition contain many foreign elements, they might not be appropriate to be used as education or clarification of the local law. Clarification of law and contribution to the science of law could then be rendered mostly or only by the academic world. Furthermore, education and social standardisation can be achieved by other means and with different approaches. The problem here will be that law's development or its analysis will be deprived from an important source of innovation and practice.

In other words, in a competitive environment adjudication risks becoming a form of arbitration. States will put adjudication in a market and treat it as a private good. Competing states will offer court adjudication to foreign parties only for dispute resolution and for cases that have little to do with their jurisdictions. This way two court adjudication functions will be lost, while the dispute resolution functions (even though regarded as a public good) will have fewer of the characteristics associated with public goods. This situation would decrease the distinction between arbitration and adjudication and would remove elements of adjudication that have been its trademark for a long time.

1.5   CONCLUSION

The relation to a *good* is subjective. What is good for someone is not a good for another. A *good* is a *public good* when it is considered as such by a government authority regardless of the opinion of private parties. In general, governments try to give non-excludable and non-rivalrous properties to public goods.

Adjudication is one of several dispute resolution mechanisms in use in many societies. It involves, among others, the use of logic, state coercion and intervention, and a dispute that is a public good. It has been considered as a public good by many governments because of its peculiarities. Adjudication has three functions that are considered as public goods: a dispute resolution function, a rule creating function and a clarification of existing laws (education) function.

There are signs of competition for adjudication in the EU. Countries have shown signs of competition and are expected to be more aggressive because of the benefits related to attracting cross-border litigants. An intensification of competition in the future can overwhelm the nature of court adjudication as a public good. Even though some of the dispute resolution function of adjudication would be formally called public goods, its nature would be private. Other elements of adjudication such as rule creation and education, and clarifying the existing law, can be detached from adjudication to make it more flexible and more manageable for competition purposes. Competition of court adjudication can make adjudication look more like arbitration and therefore more like a private good.

2 | THE (EMERGING) NEEDS FOR ADR IN RETAIL PAYMENT SYSTEMS: MEDIATION

*Safari Kasiyanto**

2.1   INTRODUCTION

"The way we pay", or what among public policy makers and in academics is known as payment systems, has developed evolutionary.[1] When fiat money[2] was introduced, people started using printing money (alongside with coins) as a means of payment to replace barter as the first fashion of exchanges.[3] The requirement for easiness and safety in payment systems has created paper-based instruments such as check and its derivatives[4] on top of banknotes and coins.[5] Afterward, triggered by the needs for efficiency in payments,[6] the popularity of paper-based instruments has been

*   Ph.D. researcher at Tilburg Law and Economic Center (TILEC) and junior research fellow at European Banking Center (EBC), Tilburg University, Warandelaan 2 5037 AB Tilburg, The Netherlands, email to S.kasiyanto@tilburguniversity.edu; Also working as a legal advisor at Bank Indonesia, the central bank of the Republic of Indonesia. The author wishes to thank Prof. Panagiotis Delimatsis for long discussions and valuable feedback, Prof. Pierre Larouche, and all participants of the 2nd Ph.D. Roundtable Forum on Law and Governance, Netherlands Institute for Law and Governance, Groningen, 4 April 2014. Special gratitude goes to Lottie Lane and team who have made this publication possible.

1.   For elaboration on the evolution of retail payment systems see for instance Committee on Payment and Settlement Systems, *Innovations in Retail Payments* (Bank for International Settlement, 2012). See also The World Bank, *Innovation in Retail Payments Worldwide: A Snapshot Outcomes of the Global Survey on Innovations in Retail Payment Instruments and Methods* (Financial Infrastructure Series, Payment Systems Policy and Research, 2012).
2.   Money printed by the authority such as the central bank, or printed by private entities appointed/approved by the authority.
3.   For development of money see for instance Dennis W Richardson, *Electronic Money: Evolution of an Electronic Funds-Transfer System* (MIT 1970). See in particular chapter two which discussed the evolution of innovation in payment systems instruments including cash, pp. 7-23. See also Thomas Greco and Vicki Robin, *Money: Understanding and Creating Alternatives to Legal Tender* (Chelsea Green Publishing Company 2001).
4.   For instance, travel checks, the checks used by travelers, and bank checks, the checks requiring its drawer to place deposit in the bank prior to the issuance of such checks.
5.   However, the trend in using checks as a means of payments is decreasing. See for instance American Banking Association, *The Changing Face of the Payments System: A Policymaker's Guide to Important Issues*, 2013, 3.
6.   Some may argue that cash is cheaper than non-cash. However, one study demonstrated that the cost in handling cash is more expensive compared to non-cash. See for instance European Central Bank and Oesterreichische National Bank, *The Future of Retail Payments: Opportunities and Challenges* (2011) and

replaced by card-based instruments such as credit cards and debit cards.[7] Lastly, people know e-money[8] and its derivatives as the most current innovative payment. Derivatives here include mobile money[9] and virtual currencies,[10] either centralized such as PayPal or decentralized such as Bitcoin.[11]

Innovation in retail payment systems has benefited consumers by providing many means of transactions faster and cheaper than those provided by traditional instruments.[12] In the end, the use of innovative payments has a significant impact on the economy. For instance, one empirical study demonstrated that electronic payments contributed to 0.3% of increase in GDP in developed economies and 0.8% of increase in GDP in emerging countries.[13] Another example is the use of mobile money in Kenya[14] that reached almost 9.5 million users in 2009, with values transacted accounting for more than USD4.26 billion in 2009, or equal to 13.33% of its national GDP, regardless there were 14.4 million unbanked adults accounted for more than 77% of all adults in the country.[15]

However, the development of retail payment systems has also brought new problems. As the relationship between payment providers and consumers is getting more

Organization for Economic Co-operation and Development, *The Future of Money* (OECD Publication Service 2002).

7. See Committee on Payment and Settlement Systems, *Innovations in Retail Payments* and The World Bank, *Innovation in Retail Payments Worldwide: A Snapshot Outcomes of the Global Survey on Innovations in Retail Payment Instruments and Methods.*

8. Electronic money or e-money is defined as monetary values stored directly or remotely in a certain medium, either card-based or server-based, including mobile money. It includes e-cash, network money, and access products whether they are tied to bank accounts or not. For a brief discussion on the definition of e-money, see for instance Safari Kasiyanto, 'E-money as Legal Tender: Does the Status really Matter?' (The 12th International Conference on e-Society 2014, Madrid, 2014).

9. Mobile money is basically server-based e-money using telecommunication technologies and mobile phone devices for transactions. A study from the International Finance Corporation (IFC) shows that mobile money is mostly used for person-to-person money transfers. See International Finance Corporation, *Mobile Money Study* (2011). In this study, IFC defines mobile money as a subset of e-money. It refers to "e-money transaction" using mobile phone. See in particular page 2 of the IFC study, discussing on Defining Mobile Money.

10. For elaboration on virtual currency, see European Central Bank, *Vitual Currency Schemes* (2012). In this study, similar to that of IFC on mobile money, the ECB also considers virtual currency as a subset of e-money. See in particular page 16 of the ECB study, discussing on Virtual Currency Schemes and E-money.

11. For discussion on Bitcoin see Sathosi Nakamoto, 'Bitcoin: A Peer-to-Peer Electronic Cash System' <http://bitcoinorg/bitcoinpdf> and <http://nakamotoinstituteorg/bitcoin/> accessed 29 October 2014. See also Joshua J Doguet, 'The Nature of the Form: Legal and Regulatory Issues Surrounding the Bitcoin Digital Currency System' (2013) 73 Louisiana Law Rev Louisiana Law Review 1119.

12. For a brief highlight on the successful use of e-money, see Kasiyanto 2014.

13. Moody's, *Moody's Analytics: The Impact of Electronic Payments on Economic Growth* (2013).

14. *M-Pesha*, which was launched in 2007.

15. International Finance Corporation, *Mobile Money Study* 18.

and more sophisticated,[16] so are the disputes arising among them. Long, exhausting and time-consuming traditional dispute resolution seems not suitable to solve such problems.[17] It then emerges the needs for alternative dispute resolution (ADR) to resolve disputes in retail payments. If adjudicative processes do not suitably resolve these disputes, which ADR will do? This paper reviews the needs for ADR to resolve disputes in retail payment systems and argues that mediation is the most suitable ADR to fill-in the needs without disturbing the existence of law and legal proceedings. To answer the question, this paper firstly uses the theoretical frameworks of payment systems to analyze the characteristics of disputes in retail payment systems.[18] It then outlines the characteristics of mediation to figure out whether mediation serves best to the characteristics of disputes in retail payment systems. In outlining the characteristics of mediation, it also compares the advantages and disadvantages of mediation with traditional adjudicative process and with other major ADR such as negotiation and arbitration. Finally, it suggests reasons why mediation fits to resolve disputes in retail payments.

2.1.1   Purpose and Previous Studies

The purpose of this article is to give recommendations on how to improve the dispute resolutions in the retail payment disputes. There are several reasons why payment systems disputes have been selected as the main topic of this article: (1) there is a significant increase of the use of retail payment systems across the world, (2) there is a rise of new types of disputes in retail payments, and (3) the main characteristics of disputes in retail payments involve only small monetary value. In addition, such disputes have also been selected as there is a phenomenon that payment systems authorities around the world have taken a similar approach in expanding the rules and regulations on payment systems, not only to cover banks but also to reach non-bank institutions (even more to non-financial institutions such as telecommunication providers). The recommendations will be useful for the authority in-charge in payment systems, such as the central bank or financial service authority, as well as authority responsible for consumer protection enforcement.

As for previous studies relating to this topic, the existing literatures can be divided into two main groups: (1) research on retail payment systems, and (2) studies on

16. For an insight on the relationship between payment systems providers and consumers, see for instance Safari Kasiyanto, *Losses from Carding: The Flaws of the Laws* (Lambert Academic Publishing 2010).
17. See for instance European Commission, *European judicial systems, Edition 2010 (data 2008): Efficiency and quality of justice* (European Judicial Systems, 2010); ADR Center, *The Cost of Non ADR – Surveying and Showing the Actual Costs of Intra-Community Commercial Litigation* (In cooperation with European Association of Craft and European Company Lawyers Association 2010); Brulard Demolin and Barthelemy, *Study on the Transparency of Costs of Civil Judicial Proceedings in the European Union* (Final Report to the European Commission, 2007).
18. Including the reasons behind the disputes and the consequences resulting from the disputes.

ADR. The main literatures in retail payment systems used as references for this paper are those introduced by international organizations or associations, and industry, having concerns in the development of payment systems. Among others are the World Bank, the Bank for International Settlement (BIS), the International Monetary Fund (IMF), central banks such as the European Central Bank (ECB), and central banks research centers such as the South East Asian Central Bank (SEACEN). Generally, these literatures can be categorized into two areas. The first area is research on how to develop national retail payment systems that consists of guidelines and minimum standards to establish sound and reliable payment systems, whereas the second area deals with innovative payments.

As for the literatures on ADR, there are a huge number of studies on this area. However, the focus of such studies is mainly on: (1) the history and the development of ADR, (2) the use of ADR to settle family, commercial, and consumer disputes, and (3) the general comparison of ADR and conventional adjudicative process. To the author's knowledge, there is no work on the use of ADR, in particular mediation, for retail payments disputes. However, some works on the use of mediation for banking disputes exist.[19] This paper will enrich the body of literatures in both retail payment systems and ADR.

2.2   RETAIL PAYMENT SYSTEMS AND DISPUTES IN RETAIL PAYMENT SYSTEMS

To have a better understanding of why the traditional adjudicative process is not suitable to resolve payment disputes, this section will outline the development of retail payment systems and the disputes arising among the parties involved. The development of retail payments will give the background on how the disputes become more and more complex, while the description of the characteristics of the retail payments disputes will help to understand why the court systems and other types of ADR are less suitable to resolve such disputes.

2.2.1   *Retail Payment Systems: Characteristics and Development*

Basically, payment systems contain two pillars: high-value[20] and retail payment systems.[21] The Bank for International Settlement (BIS) defines high-value payment systems as "payments typically of a relatively high-value and between banks and/or

---

19. See for instance Rutgers Conflict Resolution Law Journal, 'Banking on Mediator Skills' (2010) 8 Rutgers Conflict Resolution Law Journal.

20. Also known as large-value or wholesale payment systems.

21. Also known as low-value payment systems.

participants in a financial market".[22] High-value payment systems are also described as the systemically important payment systems, as any disruptions to these systems will have impact on the whole financial systems.[23] On the contrary, "retail payment systems" are defined as the systems used to process day-to-day consumers transactions.[24] This includes person-to-person transfers using all payment instruments from paper-based, card-based to electronic-based to the Internet. However, since there is a chance that consumers conduct transactions involving high-value monetary unit,[25] retail payments are usually capped to a certain value.[26]

The development of retail payments has been very impressive, as proven by statistics on the use of payment instruments.[27] As shown at **Figure 2.1**, in 2012 the value of transactions of retail payments[28] in major countries observed was tremendously exceeding cash in circulation outside the banks. Even among the countries where the people used payment instruments the least such as Sweden and Switzerland, the value of transactions was still far exceeding cash in circulation. Among the countries where the people used payment instruments the most, such as China and the UK, the value of transactions was, respectively, 170 times and 1400 times the cash in circulation.

2.2.2 Disputes in Retail Payment Systems

The rapid development of retail payment systems has a significant influence on the disputes arising among the parties involved. At the beginning of the use of payment

---

22. Committee on Payment and Settlement Systems, *General Guidance for National Payment System Development* (Bank for International Settlement, 2006). See also American Banking Association, *The Changing Face of the Payments System: A Policymaker's Guide to Important Issues*, p. 16.
23. Committee on Payment and Settlement Systems, *General Guidance for National Payment System Development*.
24. The Bank for International Settlement defines a retail payment system as *a system comprising the technical infrastructure; participants; instruments; arrangements for clearing and settlement; business relationship arrangements (such as bank-customer relationships, rules, procedures, the applicable legal framework, and governance arrangements) that, put together, provide the overall environment within which retail payments are posted, authorized, processed, cleared, and settled.* See Bank for International Settlement – Committee on Payment and Settlement Systems, *Innovations in Retail Payments*. However, this definition is not used here as it is too abstract. See also definition of retail payment systems by the European Central Bank at <www.ecb.europa.eu/paym/pol/activ/retail/html/index.en.html> last accessed on 20 August 2015.
25. For instance person-to-person transfer in order to buy a house or a land.
26. It is difficult to find evidence stating that transactions in retail payment systems are capped under certain amount. For instance, the European Central Bank only states that retail payment systems are mostly for low-value transactions (see <www.ecb.europa.eu/paym/pol/activ/retail/html/index.en.html>). However, in practice, any transaction under EUR10,000.00 is considered low-value.
27. The data used here are reproduced from data provided by CPSS. For complete statistics, see <www.bis.org/list/cpmi/tid_57/index.htm> last accessed on 20 August 2015.
28. Debit transfers, credit transfers, card payments (credit, debit, and stored-value cards), and e-money.

Figure 2.1   Comparison of value of transactions using all payment instruments, value of transactions using cards and checks, and cash in circulation outside banks (in USD bill).

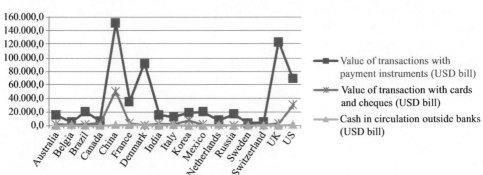

Source: CPPS, 2012.

systems, when the arrangement of transactions simply involved two direct parties,[29] the disputes arising between the parties were also simple and direct. As the retail payments have evolved, involving more and more parties and complex arrangement among them, the disputes arising are also getting more complicated. To understand why the traditional adjudicative process is not best suited to resolve disputes in retail payments, this subsection will explain the characteristics of disputes in retail payments and the consequences they brought.

There are at least seven unique characteristics[30] of disputes in retail payments. These characteristics of disputes may come from the unique characteristics of retail payment systems themselves such as two-sided market platform of payment systems[31] and the complex arrangement between the parties involved. These characteristics are described as the following.

The first is that, as having cited in the introduction, the disputes involve small monetary value only. This is generated from the fact that retail payments are used to

---

29. For instance barter between goods, or transactions using banknotes and coins.
30. There are actually plenty of small yet different characteristics of disputes in retail payments, and not necessarily always seven. As such characteristics are actually interchangeable or, sometimes, overlapping each other, merely for academic purpose this paper determines to categorize such plenty characteristics into seven distinct groups.
31. From an economic perspective payment, systems are categorized as one example of a two-sided market. This means that there are two sides of a market embedded in payment systems where pricing policy can be imposed to both sides. There are extensive literatures on the economics of a two-sided market, but for a brief (yet advanced) discussion, see for instance Jean-Charles Rochet and Jean Tirole, 'Two-sided Markets: A Progress Report' (2006) 37 The RAND Journal of Economics 645; Jean Charles Rochet and Jean Tirole, 'Tying in Two-sided Markets and the Honor All Cards Rule' (2008) 26 International Journal of Industrial Organization 1333; and also Stephen P King, 'Two-Sided Markets' (2013) 46 Australian Economic Review 247.

Figure 2.2   Total value of e-money transactions (million Eur).

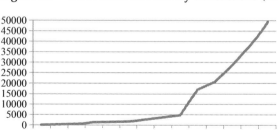

Figure 2.3   Average value of each e-money transaction (in Eur).

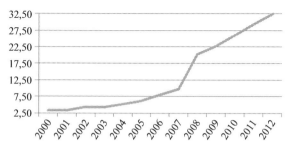

process small day-to-day transactions. To give a better understanding on how small the monetary value associated to retail payments disputes, **Figures 2.2** and **2.3** show the total value of e-money transactions and the average value of each e-money trans-action within the EU from 2000 to 2012.[32] Although the total value of e-money trans-actions significantly grew to more than EUR49billion in 2012, the average value of each transaction amounted to only EUR32.5 in 2012.[33]

The second characteristic is that a consumer facing a dispute often has to deal with many parties. In credit card transactions for instance, card holders have to deal with at least four other parties of credit card networks from merchant,[34] card issuing entity,[35] acquiring entity, and network owners such as Visa or MasterCard.[36] One rea-son why retail payment systems involve so many parties is because each system has a

---

32. Data provided here was produced from statistics available on the ECB's website (<www.ecb.europa. eu/stats/money/payments/paym/html/index.en.html>).

33. The average value of e-money transactions was simply resulted from the total value of e-money trans-actions divided by the number of e-money used. For row data visit <www.ecb.europa.eu/stats/ money/payments/paym/html/index.en.html> last accessed on 20 August 2015.

34. Merchant is the seller of goods or the provider of services from where the cardholders have purchased goods/services and to whom they have performed the transactions.

35. The entity that has issued the credit cards usually, but not always, a bank.

36. For brief yet clear elaboration on credit card transaction scheme and its development see for instance Kasiyanto 2010.

two-sided platform within its network.[37] Like many other two-sided markets, such as newspapers,[38] video game consoles,[39] or online search engines,[40] retail payment systems always consist of consumers on one side and merchants on the other side.[41]

As for the third characteristic, disputes in retail payment systems are often borderless, involving parties located in different jurisdictions. This is influenced by the extensive use of retail payments, mainly for cross-border and online transactions. In the EU for instance, the cross-border disputes have increased year after year.[42] The borderless disputes involve more sophisticated arrangements for consumers to file a complaint and therefore require closed cooperation among the relevant disputants.[43]

The fourth characteristic deals with the wide array of problems incurred in retail payment systems disputes. The problems vary, from a simple mistake in payment processing to unauthorized transactions to frauds committed from illicit activities. The World Bank in its guideline on *"developing a comprehensive national retail payment strategy"*[44] suggests that the variety of retail payment disputes can be categorized into three main groups: claims resulting from incorrect payment instructions or mistakes during the processing, losses incurred from frauds, and conflicts from operational services.[45] This grouping seems simplified, as the problems involved in each group are quite extensive. For instance, the US Consumer Financial Protection Bureau, the federal government agency responsible to tackle and resolve complaints from financial services consumers under the Dodd-Frank Act,[46] had until recently received 28,035 complaints from consumers on credit cards disputes since the agency establishment on 21 July 2011,[47] consisting of at least 15 major issues.[48] See **Figure 2.4** for details.

The fifth characteristic of retail payments disputes is that both payments users and providers are dependent on one another. From the perspective of users, there is a need

---

37. See King 2013; Sujit Chakravorti, Santiago Carbo-Valverde, and Francisco Rodriguez-Fernandez, 'Regulating Two-sided Markets: An Empirical Investigation' (European Central Bank, 2009).

38. Readers and advertisers.

39. Gamers and game developers.

40. Internet users and advertisers.

41. For good elaboration on two-sided market of payment systems see also Julian Wright, 'Why Payment Card Fees are Biased against Retailers' (2012) 43 The RAND Journal of Economics 761.

42. See European Commission, *FIN-NET Activity Report 2011* (Financial Institutions, Retail financial services and consumer policy, 2012).

43. Elizabeth Parushkova, 'Home Country Ombudsman Scheme: Cooperation with Other National ADRs through Fin Net' (Workshop on Consumer Dispute Resolution in Financial Market, Ankara, 4 May 2010).

44. The World Bank, *Developing a Comprehensive National Payment Systems Strategy* (Final print-ready version, 2012).

45. Ibid 49-50.

46. See Dodd-Frank Act, Section 1021(c)(2).

47. Consumer Financial Protection Bureau, *Consumer Response: A Snapshot of Complaints Received* (2013).

48. For detail data please visit CFPB's website: Source: <https://data.consumerfinance.gov/>.

Figure 2.4   Issues involved in credit card complaints received by the US Consumer Financial Protection Bureau, 2011–2014.

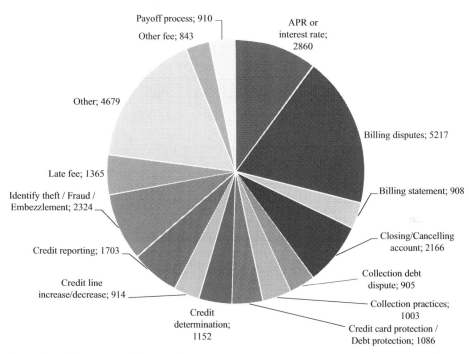

Source: https://data.consumerfinance.gov/.

to keep using similar payment services in the (immediate) future. This applies vice versa to the payments providers as they also have a great interest to keep the users loyal. This relationship dependence requires both parties to employ resolutions in a manner consistent with their interests, keeping confidentiality as one of the top priorities and a win-win solution as the ultimate goal.

As for the sixth characteristic, disputes in retail payment systems are often caused by the lack of information or awareness of the consumers. This problem occurs not only from the ignorance of the consumers but perhaps also because of the growing numbers of new payment products.[49] This condition could lead to the consumer's confusion as they do not know or are even aware of how to file a complaint. Well-informed dispute resolution is emerging to resolve this case. For the payment system industry, consumers who are enriched with information on rights and obligations are important to discipline the markets and create competition among the providers. In the end, this will lead to offering better products by the providers.[50]

---

49. See for instance Ronald J Mann, *Charging Ahead: The Growth and Regulation of Payment Card Markets* (Cambridge University Press 2007). In this book, Mann highlights conditions in card payment that lead to the banks keep charging the consumers with fees and expenses.
50. The World Bank, *Developing a Comprehensive National Payment Systems Strategy*.

Lastly, the characteristic of disputes in retail payment systems shares the common characteristic of general consumer disputes. The disputes arise in a condition that the bargaining position of users and providers is unequal. Users are usually individuals whereas providers are commonly big firms in payment networks, from multinational entities (network owners such as Visa or MasterCard in credit cards), to national companies (global banks) to retailers (merchants such as Carrefour or Wal-Mart). This unequal bargaining position leads to the need for specific arrangement of dispute resolution that not only satisfies the giant parties but also protects the interest of the small consumers.

2.3   ADR AND MEDIATION AS ADR

2.3.1   *Scope and Definition of ADR*

Despite the debate over the term "alternative" used in ADR,[51] one example of a simple yet clear definition of ADR is "a broad spectrum of structured processes, including mediation and reconciliation, which does not include litigation though it may be linked to or integrated with litigation, and which involves the assistance of a neutral third party, and which empowers parties to resolve their own disputes".[52] Another definition was introduced by the European Commission on its green paper on ADR.[53] In this paper, the European Commission defined ADR as "...out-of-court dispute resolution processes conducted by a neutral third party, excluding arbitration".[54] From such definitions, it implies that ADR is a sort of umbrella term covering a number of out-of-court dispute resolution processes that differ in terms of formality levels, the involvement of third party and its role, the legal status of the outcome and its enforceability.

2.3.2   *ADR Roles in a Modern Civil Justice System*

Although courts will remain the center of the civil judicial system serving as a sort of forum of the last resort, the recognition of ADR in many jurisdictions across the world is continuously growing.[55] The relationship between ADR and court-based

---

51. Sir Laurence Street, the former Chief Justice of New South Wales, in Lewis and McCrimmon, *The Role of ADR Processes in the Criminal Justice System: A View from Australia*, available at <www.justice.gov.za> commented that the term "alternative" is not appropriate to name after dispute resolution mechanism outside the court. He proposed to use the term "additional".
52. Law Reform Commission, *Alternative Dispute Resolution: Mediation and Conciliation* (2010) 13.
53. European Commission, *Green Paper on Alternative Dispute Resolution in Civil and Commercial Law* (2002).
54. This definition was to promote the use of ADR other than arbitration to resolve disputes in civil and commercial law, in-line with the purpose of the green paper. However, the coverage of ADR in this paper includes arbitration.
55. Nadja Alexander, *Global Trends in Mediation* (second edn, Kluwer Law International 2006).

settlement is complex and evolving.[56] However, both should be seen as an integrated part.[57] ADR and conventional adjudicative processes are heterogeneous but not-separated and not opposed entities.

In modern society, high-quality legal services are important,[58] yet the availability of such services is very limited because conventional adjudicative process such as courts is costly and cumbersome.[59] That is why the European Commission, for instance, emphasized that member states are obliged to provide access to justice by providing swift and low-cost legal proceedings in each member state.[60] One way to fill-in the needs of access to justice is to recognize and employ ADR to resolve certain cases without disturbing the existence of judicial proceedings.

One might argue that by employing ADR to resolve certain cases,[61] it has the meaning that access to justice has been increased is overwhelming.[62] The parties resolving the disputes may not consider themselves as receiving justice but modestly regard it as settling their disputes. However, some others[63] have also suggested that increasing access to justice is not only about increasing access to the justice institutions but also giving people more choice in resolving their disputes and more appropriate forum to resolve each dispute.[64]

2.3.3 *Mediation as ADR: Definition and Advantages*

The EU Directive on mediation defines mediation as "… a structured process, however named or referred to, whereby two or more parties to a dispute attempt by themselves, on a voluntary basis, to reach an agreement on the settlement of their dispute with the assistance of a mediator."[65] It is originally and generally used to resolve disputes in family law, commercial, and property.

---

56. Robert M Goldschmid, *Major Themes of Civil Justice Reform* (Discussion Paper, Prepared for the Civil Justice Reform Working Group, 2006).
57. Law Reform Commission, *Alternative Dispute Resolution: Mediation and Conciliation* 8.
58. Civil Justice Reform Working Group, *Green Paper: The Foundations of Civil Justice Reform* (2004).
59. European Commission, *European judicial systems, Edition 2010 (data 2008): Efficiency and quality of justice*; ADR Center, *The Cost of Non ADR – Surveying and Showing the Actual Costs of Intra-Community Commercial Litigation*; Demolin, *Study on the Transparency of Costs of Civil Judicial Proceedings in the European Union*.
60. European Commission, *Green Paper on Alternative Dispute Resolution in Civil and Commercial Law* (2002).
61. For instance small cases.
62. South African Law Commission, *Alternative Dispute Resolution* (1997).
63. Law Reform Commission, *Report on Mediation and Conciliation in Commercial Matters* (2010).
64. Law Reform Commission, *Alternative Dispute Resolution: Mediation and Conciliation* 9.
65. Article 3a Directive 2008/52/EC of the European Parliament and of the Council of 21 May 2008 on certain aspects of mediation in civil and commercial matters.

As for the advantages of mediation, there are great numbers of literatures mentioning on the advantages of mediation.[66] To summarize,[67] the benefits in using mediation include lowercost, faster process, quality for using skilled mediator, flexibility, predictable outcome, win-win solution,[68] controllable by involving parties, confidential process,[69] limited risk since the process focuses to the party's interests, maintaining the relationship between the disputed parties,[70] and involving minimum liability or no pressure to reach any decisions.[71]

2.3.4   Mediation Processes

If ADR is a sort of umbrella term, the term of mediation shares the same function but with a narrower coverage. For instance, one can look at the scope and the models of mediation. The scope of mediation can be divided into two general types: a day-to-day negotiation conducted by a third party to resolve a dispute[72] and a more structured procedure which is regulated and governed by ground rules.[73] As for the models of mediation, there are several models to mediate, from facilitative[74] to evaluative[75] and from transformative[76] to therapeutic. There is also system design

---

66. See for instance Alexander 2006; Burcu Savun, 'Information, Bias, and Mediation Success' (2008) 52 International Studies Quarterly 25; European Commission, *Report on Mediation and Conciliation in Commercial Matters*; James C Freund, 'Three's a Crowd-How to Resolve a Knotty Multi-Party Dispute Through Mediation' (2009) 64 The Business Lawyer 359; Rebecca Attree, '(1) The impact of the EU Mediation Directive: a United Kingdom Perspective, (2) Essential Skills of Mediation for Lawyers' (A paper prepared for the Libralex Meeting, Perugia, 22 October 2011); and International Finance Corporation, *Alternative Dispute Resolution Program (ADR) in THE Western Balkans: Giving Mediation a Chance, Telling Our ADR Story* (IFC Advisory Services in partenrship with the Kingdom of the Netherlands, 2010).
67. This summary is mainly based on a study by Eric M Runesson and Marie-Laurence Guy, *Mediating Corporate Governance Conflicts and Disputes* (Global Corporate Governance Forum 2007).
68. See Felix Steffek, *Mediation in the European Union* (An Introduction to European Commission, 2012) 13. In this article, Steffek uses the terms "sustainable and just solutions".
69. See also Steven Friel and Christian Toms, 'The European Mediation Directive-Legal and Political Support for Alternative Dispute Resolution in Europe' (2011) Bloomberg Law Reports.
70. Australian Government, *Resolution of Small Business Disputes* (Option paper, 2011) 3.
71. Steffek, *Mediation in the European Union* 10. In this article, Steffek states that in mediation "parties only agree if they really want the solution..." For the complete benefits of mediation as summarized here, See Guy, *Mediating Corporate Governance Conflicts and Disputes* 25.
72. This is very general coverage as in this sense mediation can cover any types of negotiation conducted by any individual to resolve any issues. In most occasions, even the parties do not realize that they are in the state of performing a mediation.
73. This is a more institutional mediation in the sense that the processes will follow the formal steps that have been previously agreed. This paper deals with this kind of mediation.
74. In this sense, the mediator only plays a role as a facilitator among the parties to reach an agreement. She has neither the power to force the parties to reach any decisions nor the authority to make any decisions.
75. Not only facilitating, the mediator also has a power or duty to evaluate the case.
76. Transformative mediation has a certain objective in which the agreement reached by the parties aims to alter one condition into another condition, hopefully a better one.

approach mediation[77] and heart-based approach mediation.[78] The latter is mostly used to settle family disputes.

The next question arises of how to initiate mediation, and what the procedures to follow in order to settle disputes via mediation are. In general, five main processes must be taken in settling disputes through mediation.[79] The first procedure is that both parties must agree to voluntarily enter into the mediation process. This can be a double-edged sword in settling disputes. On one side, the voluntary process can be a benefit if both disputants have a good will to settle disputes, but on the other side it can prevent the parties to reach a resolution if they have no good intention.[80] An example of a bad intention is when one party has agreed to mediate but has no actual intention to resolve the problem. This, for instance, could happen because the intention of that party to mediate is driven by "external forces" such as reputation or regulation. The second step is selecting the mediator. Both parties must agree to select the mediator to facilitate the process, and it must be ensured that the mediator selected is neutral and that it is in the best interest to entourage the disputants to reach an agreement. The next steps are making initial contact with the mediator to set up a first meeting, exchange any documents or information, problem identification if necessary, and negotiation. The latter procedure is the core process of mediation, in which the parties involved exchange their views, discuss their interests, and search for the best, win-win solution. If the negotiation works well, the parties will reach a settlement. The complete processes of mediation is outlined in **Figure 2.5**.

2.3.5   Limitations of Mediation

Mediation is not one-size-fits-all dispute resolution or a panacea for all disputes.[81] Mediation might have been compromised and therefore lack some of its benefits if both parties do not have a good and genuine faith to resolve dispute. If this is the case, some advantages of mediation such as flexibility, full control by the parties, voluntary-based process, and minimum liability will turn mediation into the weakest resolution mechanism. It will then be very difficult to reach settlement in mediation. The mediation process will become costly and cumbersome, making it into a sort of additional layer to civil litigation.

---

77. This most likely has a structured, formal process.
78. See International Institute for Conflict Prevention & Resolution (1998), *Mediation Procedure: CPR Procedures and Clauses*, CPR International Institute for Conflict Prevention & Resolution.
79. Law Reform Commission, *Alternative Dispute Resolution: Mediation and Conciliation* (2010).
80. See discussion on Section 2.3.5 "Limitations of Mediation".
81. See for instance Warren K Winkler, 'Access to Justice, Mediation: Panacea or Pariah?' (2007) 16 Canadian Arbitration and Mediation Journal 5. Also available at <www.ontariocourts.on.ca/coa/en/ps/speeches/access.htm>.

Figure 2.5   Mediation processes.

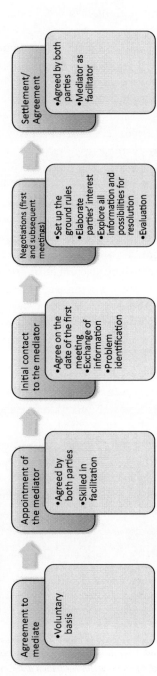

Source: World Intellectual Property Organization International (WIPO) Alternative Dispute Resolution (ADR) for ITPGRFA Standard Material Transfer Agreement, <www.wipo.int/amc/en/center/specific-sectors/biodiversity/itpgrfa/>; and the International Institute for Conflict Prevention and Resolution, *Mediation Procedure: CPR Procedures and Clauses* (CPR International Institute for Conflict Prevention & Resolution 1998), simplified.

2.4   THE USE OF MEDIATION AS ADR TO RESOLVE DISPUTES IN RETAIL
             PAYMENT SYSTEMS

2.4.1   *The Disadvantages of Conventional Adjudicative Process Compared to*
             Mediation

Compared to mediation, the conventional adjudicative process contains mainly three problems in solving retail payment systems disputes: cost problem, time-consuming problem, and substance problem.

The cost problem comes from the most unique characteristic of retail payment systems: it is used for small value payments only.[82] From economic point of views, it is not worth doing for consumers to go before the court to solve the disputes they face for the total cost in doing so will far exceed the value of the payment itself. The next problem, which is a time-consuming problem, is associated with the fact that the traditional adjudicative process is usually long and cumbersome. As for the substance problems, it has been explained that a dispute in retail payment systems is minor harm or small claim, so according to the theory of allocation of scarcity resource it is not wise to allocate the limited legal experts such as judges or attorneys to solve the minor problems. In addition, there is also concern related to the relationship of consumers and service providers in retail payment systems. Consumers of retail payments are often dependent on the service providers for using the next products or services.[83] It also applies vice versa to the payments providers, in which they have a great interest to keep their customers loyal. Thus, solving the disputes without disturbing the relationship between consumers and providers is essential to keep the confidence of consumers of retail payments and the sustainability of the payment systems providers.[84] The meta-comparison between the traditional adjudicative process and mediation to resolve payment systems disputes is outlined in **Figure 2.6**.

2.4.2   *The Benefits of Mediation Compared to Other Types of ADR in Resolving*
             Payment Systems Disputes

Citing from the Irish Law Reform Commission's report on mediation and conciliation as ADR,[85] two elements could be employed to assess why a certain mechanism of ADR serves best to resolve a certain dispute, prevailing over the other types of ADR. The first is *how such mechanism suits best to serve the specific interests of the parties,*

---

82. Bruce J Summers, *Payment Systems: Design, Governance and Oversight* (Central Banking Publications 2012); The World Bank, *Innovation in Retail Payments Worldwide: A Snapshot Outcomes of the Global Survey on Innovations in Retail Payment Instruments and Methods.*
83. The World Bank, *The Future of Retail Payments: Opportunities and Challenges.*
84. See The World Bank, *Developing a Comprehensive National Payment Systems Strategy.*
85. European Commission, *Alternative Dispute Resolution: Mediation and Conciliation.*

Figure 2.6   Meta-comparison between traditional adjudicative process and mediation to resolve payment systems disputes.

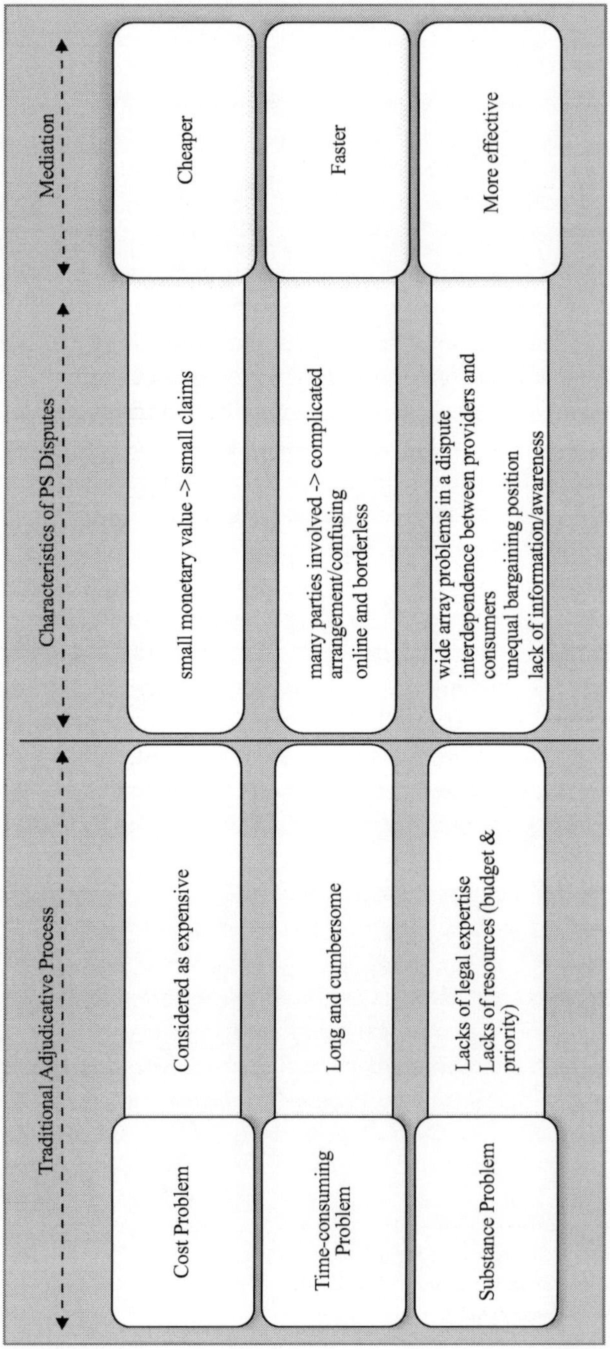

Traditional Adjudicative Process		Characteristics of PS Disputes	Mediation
Cost Problem	Considered as expensive	small monetary value -> small claims	Cheaper
Time-consuming Problem	Long and cumbersome	many parties involved -> complicated arrangement/confusing online and borderless	Faster
Substance Problem	Lacks of legal expertise Lacks of resources (budget & priority)	wide array problems in a dispute interdependence between providers and consumers unequal bargaining position lack of information/awareness	More effective

Source: Author.

and the second is *how such mechanism suits best to ensure that justice is accessible, efficient, and effective for the parties involved*.[86] In using those two elements, the characteristics of mediation must always be borne in mind.[87]

2.4.2.1   How Mediation Is Most Suitable to Serve the Specific Interests of Both Disputing Parties

In order to answer this question, it is necessary to once again recall the seven characteristics of disputes in retail payments because such characteristics contain the specific interests from both disputing parties.[88] These specific interests are generated by analyzing the reasons behind such characteristics of disputes and then looking for the direct consequences resulting from such characteristics. Once the direct consequences are generated, it becomes much easier to draw what the specific interests of the parties actually are. For instance, from the characteristic that the disputes only involve small monetary value, it can be concluded that the characteristic comes from the nature of retail payment transactions, used only to perform small daily transactions. This leads to a direct consequence that the disputes are only minor harms/small claims which will not be worth litigating or arbitrating. Therefore, the specific interest drawn from this characteristic is the need for a simple, customized yet expedited dispute resolution system. All characteristics of disputes in retail payments have been analyzed using this method, and such analysis is provided in **Table 2.1**.

As outlined in **Table 2.1**, the first group of specific interests of both disputants consists of the needs for a simple, customized, simplified yet expedited, win-win solution and well-informed dispute resolution process. These needs come from the characteristics of retail payment disputes in that they only involve small values of money but deal with many parties, and the lack of information or awareness of the consumers. Because the disputes involve only small amounts of money, they are not worth settling through an arbitration process, for the cost of arbitration is likely to be beyond the dispute's value. For example, most of us would agree that it is not worth doing to bring a dispute on an e-money transaction in Europe before the arbitration tribunal, for the value of e-money transactions is on average only EUR32.[89]

Besides mediation, negotiation may suffice to resolve disputes involving small monetary value. However, significant problems may be faced in dealing with the other two factors: the involvement of many parties during disputes and the lack of awareness of consumers. Since there are at least two payment providers involved in every payment system dispute, negotiation to resolve dispute would be impracticable. For instance,

---

86. Ibid 10-11.
87. See Steffek, *Mediation in the European Union* 4-5.
88. For the detail, see Section 4.2.2.
89. See description on the development of payment systems and chart in **Figure 2.3**.

Table 2.1   How characteristics of retail payments disputes lead to the interests of disputants.

No	Characteristics of Retail Payments Disputes		Consequences	
	Characteristics	**Reasons**	**Direct Consequences**	**Specific Interests**
1.	Involving small monetary value	Resulted from • Small daily payments • Mass transactions	Minor harms/small claims, not worth for litigation or arbitration.	Need for a simple, customized yet expedited dispute resolution
2.	Involving many parties	Payment system is two-sided market	Complicated arrangement to complaint	Simplified dispute resolution procedures
3.	Often borderless	Cross-border and online transactions	More effort to be settled	Cooperation among parties in different jurisdictions
4.	Wide array of problems, from simple mistaken in payment processing to frauds from illicit activities	• Extensive use • Advance technology adoption in payment systems (innovative payments)	The needs of wide array of (specific) expertize	Competence and neutral third party
5.	Both consumers and payment services providers are dependent to each other	Consumers need to keep using the payment services in the future while payment service providers have interest to keep the customers loyal	Win-win but executable dispute resolution	Mediation
6.	Unequal bargaining position	Customer vs. payment service provider network (typical consumer disputes)	Need for specific arrangement of dispute resolutions	Obligatory dispute resolution mechanism
7.	Lack of information or awareness of consumers	• Ignorance • Great numbers of new products/services	Consumers do not know how to resolve their problems	Well-informed dispute resolution

Source: Author.

when a consumer of card payments[90] has a dispute relating to his transaction, he has to deal with at least four parties: the merchant (retailer), issuer (bank), acquirer (also bank), and card network owner (principal). It would be unrealistic for the consumer alone to negotiate with these four "giant" parties. Thus, the need for a third neutral yet competent party to facilitate the dispute resolution emerges.

The second group of interests from disputants consists of two elements. As just mentioned, the first is the need for a third neutral and competent party to facilitate the dispute resolution, while the second is the need for cooperation among parties in different jurisdictions. The need for a third neutral and competent party comes from the

90. Not necessarily credit card scheme. It could be debit card, prepaid, or even mobile money.

fact that disputes in retail payments contain a wide array of problems, from simple mistakes in payment systems to fraudulent or illicit activities.[91] Mediation serves best to resolve these disputes because it has the similar advantage to that of negotiation in term of having interest-based mechanism, and it shares the benefit of arbitration in term of employing third neutral party. On the other hand, cooperation among parties in different jurisdictions to resolve disputes in payment systems is needed as payment transactions are now getting borderless.

The third interest is rather tricky, which is the need for an obligatory dispute resolution mechanism. As self-explanatory from the text, this need is basically against the nature of mediation, which requires the parties to voluntarily agree to resolve disputes using mediation process. However, the need for an obligatory dispute resolution only arises when one disputant rejects the agreement to mediate offered by the other disputant. This may be the case for regular consumer disputes but is most likely not the case for payment systems disputes as both disputants are dependent to use each other service. Why does this seem not applicable to payment systems disputes? This issue will be elaborated in detail on the next subsection.[92] However, if this is the case, there is an emerging need to create a sort of "obligatory" mediation.[93] The obligation part of this mechanism covers only the enforcement to the refusing party to agree to mediate, whereas the whole process of mediation itself remains voluntary.

2.4.2.2 *How Mediation Is Most Suitable to Ensure That Justice Is Accessible, Efficient, and Effective for the Parties Involved*

The key element of this question is whether or not mediation[94] has the ability to ensure that justice is: (1) accessible to the disputants, (2) efficient in terms of time and resource allocation, and (3) effective in resolving such disputes. In order to answer this question, first we need to look at the distinctions between each type of ADR as described in **Figure 2.7**.

The types of ADR selected in this paper are negotiation, mediation, and arbitration.[95] The distinctions between each type are measured by the time devotion, resource (cost, human resource) allocation, party control, and the flexibility of each resolution

---

91. See detail discussion on sub section on the characteristics of payment systems disputes.
92. Subsection on how mediation suits best to ensure that justice is accessible, efficient, and effective for the parties involved that comes right after this discussion.
93. In this case, arbitration is still less tempting considering the other important characteristics of payment systems disputes, i.e., involving small monetary value.
94. Compared to other types of ADR.
95. As well-known, there are many other types of ADR beside these three, such as quasi-mediation arbitration, conciliation, obligatory mediation, and so on. However, for the sake of conciseness, this paper only compared mediation to negotiation and arbitration as both the later types represent the most and the least type of ADR in terms of time and resource allocation, party control, and flexibility of the process.

Figure 2.7   **Distinctions between each dispute resolution under ADR.**[96]

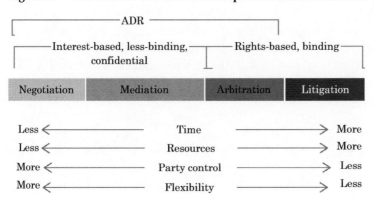

process on the one hand, and whether it is interest-based or rights-based, confidential, and binding on the other hand. For time devotion and resource allocation, arbitration requires the most, whereas negotiation demands the least.[97] Mediation in this context places in the middle. It requires a shorter time and less resources compared to arbitration, but needs more time and resource allocation compared to negotiation. As for party control and flexibility, arbitration is the least flexible, whereas negotiation is the most flexible. Again, mediation remains in the middle between arbitration and negotiation. Mediation is nearly as flexible as negotiation, but has the advantages of arbitration in terms of having a third neutral party to facilitate the dispute resolution. Another characteristic is that both negotiation and mediation are interest-based, whereas arbitration is more righ to bligation based. It is also believed that information generated or occurred during negotiation or mediation processes is more confidential, although the agreement reached in both types of ADR is less binding than that resulted from arbitration.

To figure out whether or not mediation is best in ensuring the accessibility, the efficiency and the effectiveness of justice, we analyzed the characteristics of disputes in retail payments against the advantages or disadvantages of each from the three types ADR. Such an analysis is shown at **Figure 2.8**. To determine the accessibility of justice, we use the party control and the flexibility of the dispute resolution processes, while to measure the efficiency of justice we use the time devotion and resource allocation. Lastly, interest vs. rights-based, binding vs. less-binding,[98] and the confidentiality of

---

96. Summarized from Lukasz Rozdeiczer and Alejandro Alvarez de la Campa, *Alternative Dispute Resolution Manual: Implementing Commercial Mediation* (IFC 2006).
97. In this context, litigation is not relevant since the analysis of this subsection focuses on the comparison among types of ADR. See previous subsection for comparison of mediation to litigation.
98. The term "less-binding" is used here merely for the sake of comparison among the three types of ADR. It does not necessarily mean that the agreement reached by negotiation or mediation, for instance, is not binding. Under most laws in many jurisdictions, well-known as "pacta sunt servanda", an agreement is

Figure 2.8   Mapping of the characteristics of disputes in retail payments among the types of ADR.

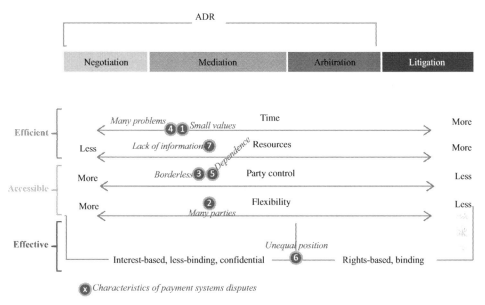

the ADR are used to determine the effectiveness of the justice, as these three characteristics have a great amount of influence on whether an ADR is more or less
enforceable.

The first measurement is that mediation should promote the accessibility of justice. To
determine this, we use party control and the flexibility of the mediation process compared to negotiation and arbitration. The relevant characteristics of payment disputes
in this case are the involvement of many parties, the online and borderless transactions,
and the dependence between consumers and providers to use each other's services in
the immediate future. As previously outlined, party control and flexibility in mediation
is in the middle position between negotiation and arbitration. It is more flexible and
involves more control from the disputants compared to arbitration, but is not as loose
as the negotiation processes. As the parties involved in payment systems disputes are
many and varied, resulting from the two-sided market, it is essential to give enough,

---

binding to the parties involved. Hence, less-binding here could be interpreted in two manners: process
and enforceability. Process in negotiation and mediation is more flexible compared to that of arbitration.
Parties have more control to initiate, negotiate, and reach any agreements, whereas in arbitration there is
a third party (individual or tribunal) who acts as a judge. In negotiation and mediation, parties involved
have an option to opt out anytime they want. This is not always the case in arbitration. As for the
enforceability, agreement reached by negotiation and mediation is, again using the term "less-", less-
enforceable compared to that of arbitration (or litigation). It is enforceable but not directly. The unsatis-
fied party needs to go before the court to get the agreement enforced.

but not too much, flexibility and more party control in order to make the dispute resolution work best. Too much room in flexibility and party control may lead to confusion
among the parties and make it even harder for them to reach a decision/agreement.
This is also the case considering that disputes in payment systems often involve online
and borderless transactions. As highlighted in the development of retail payments, the
use of online and cross-border transactions tends to hike up. These transactions involve
more and more jurisdictions, so it becomes more difficult for disputants to seek resolution. Employing arbitration would be too expensive, and using negotiation would be
too difficult as there is a need for a coordinator to resolve the disputes. Thus, online
mediation would be the best way to resolve this kind of disputes.

The second assessment is whether mediation promotes the efficiency of justice. In this
context, the most relevant characteristics of ADR are time devotion and resource alloca-
tions, while the relevant characteristics of payment disputes namely are small monetary
values involved, the variety of the problems, and the lack of information or awareness
from the consumers. As general principles, it would greatly benefit both disputants if
they could spend as little time as possible in settling disputes, and to allocate resources
such as cost and human resources as low as possible. Thus, the most proper ADR type to
choose is either negotiation or mediation. Arbitration would be out in the context of
resource allocation as it is much more expensive compared to the other two. In the context
of time devotion, one may argue that arbitration is as efficient as mediation. However,
looking at the fact that the nature of arbitration is to process the dispute settlement more
formally, arbitration could be more cumbersome. In addition, mediation has advantages
in speeding up the process if both disputants initiate the process with good will.

It then comes to a choice between mediation and negotiation. In general, negotiation
might require less time and resource allocation than mediation does. However, as previously mentioned, mediation shares the advantage of arbitration that negotiation
does not, in terms of having a third neutral party to facilitate the dispute settlement
processes. Most negotiation does not have this advantage, as it is basically a forum
where direct meetings between disputants take place to reach a common interest. Furthermore, unequal bargaining position between consumers and payment providers
as another characteristic of payment disputes could deteriorate the use of negotiation
to resolve payment disputes. As the bargaining position between consumers on one
side (mainly individuals) and payment providers on the other side (mainly big firms
and retailers) is significantly unequal, the benefits of negotiation having a shorter time
span and resource allocation could be hindered. In this case, both disputants might
face difficulties in reaching a common goal. Considering these circumstances, mediation is the optimum way to promote the efficiency of justice.

The last dimension to assess is whether or not mediation ensures the effectiveness of
justice. How can this be determined? Mediation is basically interest-based and confidential process. Logically, this type of process attracts more and more people to

resolve their problems. As it is interest-based, the chance to reach an agreement is higher than that of a decisive process based on rights and obligations of the parties. Statistics show that most disputes processed through mediation are resolved. However, there are also flaws coming from the use of mediation to resolve disputes in payment systems. As one of the characteristics of payment systems disputes is the unequal bargaining position of the disputants, it might be very difficult to start the mediation process considering the fact that the most fundamental nature of mediation is the voluntariness of the process. Theoretically, payment providers as the stronger party are more likely to refuse the agreement to mediate if they do not observe any chances of getting benefits.

However, in practice, not all payment providers reject the agreement to mediate in the first place. As more and more information on the benefits of mediation is disbursed, business entities become more curious in digging-in on the further information on how mediation could solve their problems and therefore help their business grows. Specifically for payment systems businesses, there are a number of arguments as to why settling their consumer's disputes is essential. First, back to the conditions that the payment providers are basically dependent on the same customers for using their other products in the immediate future. From an economic perspective of two-sided market and network industry, this is known as consumers being "locked-in" to a certain product. For instance, it is essential for a bank issuing credit cards to keep their customers "locked-in" to use the same credit card and not to move to another credit card issued by another bank. In this sense, they realize that maintaining their customers is essential to support their business sustainability. Second, as payment providers are bound to their consumers, reputation and consumer satisfaction are to some extent accounted more in payment systems business.

Those two arguments convince payment systems providers that providing practical dispute resolution for consumers has more positive impact to their business. That is the reason why some payment providers have even created their own dispute resolution mechanism. The best example of this private dispute resolution is best represented by "the credit card charge back mechanism" introduced by the credit card network. Under this mechanism, a credit card user who is disputing a certain transaction may file a complaint to seek redress. After a series of investigation, the credit card issuer will deliver the outcome in which it may refund the money (so-called charge back) or withhold the complaint. Although this mechanism is, of course, not mediation, the willingness of payment systems providers to settle disputes is clearly significant. Thus, the theory stating that the payment systems provider as the stronger party would be more likely to reject the agreement to mediate is simply exaggerated.

To summarize, mediation clearly ensures the effectiveness of justice by providing alternative dispute resolution, side by side with negotiation and arbitration.

Generated from the nature of mediation, which is interest-based and confidential dispute resolution, statistics show that the success rate of mediation is quite high.

2.4.3   Challenges

The challenges in applying mediation to resolve retail payment systems disputes come from two areas: (1) the readiness of the retail payment systems industry, and (2) readiness of the mediation experts.

The readiness of the retail payment industry covers both sides of the markets: the consumers and the providers. As for the consumers, the best way to introduce mediation is by providing concise yet clear information on what mediation is, what the advantages and disadvantages are, and some other practical knowledge on how to use mediation.[99] As for the payment systems providers, in 2009 the Internal Market and Services DG of the EU Commission reported[100] that there was a going concern from the financial services providers in dealing with the costs of having certain ADR schemes to resolve the dispute in financial services. Their ongoing concern was that the costs incurred in having such ADR schemes to resolve financial services disputes should not outweigh their advantages.[101] This is understandable since the focus of the providers is more profit oriented, to generate more income. Thus, cost always becomes their primary concern. However, this concern may not overweigh the promotion of ADR to resolve payment systems disputes (or financial services disputes) for two reasons. First, from a strategic management point of view, employing ADR to replace court settlement (or litigation) in setting up the legal strategy of companies is less costly. ADR predicts more precisely the outcome of the dispute resolution and more easily calculates the cost compared to court settlement. Overall, ADR gives rise to companies controlling the outcome and the cost of dispute settlement. Second, the concern of the providers in this matter is not only against to the consumer interests but also social welfare. When it comes to social welfare, and when the concern of the providers is against such a purpose, there is a need to adjust the providers' concern to achieve optimum equilibrium of the market.

The next challenge deals with readiness of the mediation experts. This includes the strategy to overcome the lack of resources, how to conduct the training and to gain the commitment of skilled mediators who have a good understanding both of

---

99.   Good information on how to provide information on ADR has been reported by FIN-NET in term of explaining and using ADR as resolution to tackle cross-border disputes. See European Commission, *Evaluation of FIN-NET* (Financial Institutions, Retail financial services and consumer policy, 2009) Commission, *FIN-NET activity report 2011*.

100. In term of using ADR to resolve disputes in financial services.

101. European Commission, *Summary of the Responses to the Public Consultation on Alternative Dispute Resolution in the Area of Financial Services* (Financial Institutions: Retail issues, consumer policy and payment systems, 2009).

mediation processes and payment systems disputes.[102] This challenge has been clai-
med as the major cause of why mediation has not generally flourished in Europe.

2.5   CONCLUSIONS

Every single dispute in retail payment systems has at least one of the following
characteristics:
• involving small monetary value but most likely many parties,
• often borderless,
• having wide array of problems from simple mistaken in payment processing to
  fraud,
• great dependence of consumers to payment systems providers and vice versa,
• unequal bargaining position, and
• lack of information or awareness of the consumers.

These characteristics come from the exceptional functions and arrangements of retail
payment systems: they are used to process small day-to-day payments only, the two-
sided markets of payment systems, the extensive use of retail payments for cross-border and online transactions, the adoption of advanced technology and innovation, the
interests of consumers and providers to keep using each others' services, the ignorance of the consumers and the great numbers of new products that can lead to confusion. Conventional adjudicative processes do not serve these disputes the best as
there would be problems incurred in employing court litigation, namely, cost problems, time-consuming problems, and substance problems. Thus, the need for ADR to
resolve payment system disputes is emerging.

Mediation stands out amongst the two other types of ADR, negotiation and arbitration, to resolve disputes in retail payment systems. This is based on the assessment
conducted using two key questions: whether mediation serves best the interests of
the disputing parties, and whether mediation suits best in ensuring the accessibility,
the efficiency and the effectiveness of justice. After analyzing the interests of both disputants generated from the characteristics of disputes in retail payments, it was found
that mediation is the optimum way to resolve such disputes as its benefits would protect the interests of both disputants. The benefits include lower-costs, a faster process,
flexible arrangements and more control by disputing parties, a predictable outcome, a
win-win solution, a confidential process and limited risks since the process focuses on
the parties' interests and maintaining the relationship between the disputing parties.
Furthermore, those advantages of mediation will also help in ensuring the accessibility, the efficiency, and the effectiveness of justice. However, considering the fact that

---

102. See European Commission, *FIN-NET activity report 2011.*

disputes in retail payment systems is a subset of consumer disputes in which consumers and payment providers often have unequal bargaining position, in theory,
mediation might face a problem being implemented if the payment providers (as
the stronger party) have no intention to mediate. This theory generally applies to most
consumer disputes. However, in practice, this theory is not applicable to payment systems disputes for two reasons. Firstly, as the transaction performed in a retail payment is not an outright transaction, the relationship between payment providers
and consumers tends to be more long lasting. In this case, the payment providers need
to "lock-in" their consumers as they will use the products over and over again in the
future. Secondly, as the payment providers are bound to their consumers, their reputation and consumer satisfaction are more important in payment systems business.
Those two arguments convince payment systems providers that providing practical
dispute resolution for consumers has more positive impact on their business. In reality, some payment providers such as credit card networks even provide their own
dispute resolution mechanism, such as the so-called "the credit card charge back
mechanism". Considering this circumstance, the proposal to apply mediation to
resolve retail payment systems disputes remains valid.

2.6   FURTHER RESEARCH

The findings of this research can be strengthened by conducting empirical research
such as surveys to consumers and payment providers on resolving payment systems
disputes using ADR,[103] discussing the use of mediation as ADR to resolve banking
consumer disputes since there is an overlap between banking products and payment
systems services, and elaborating the practical issues in implementing mediation to
resolve payment systems disputes.

---

103. Both implementations and perception. Surveys on implementation is useful to discover the facts,
     whereas on perception can predict the future of the ADR.

3 | FROM DISPUTE SETTLEMENT TO JUDICIAL REVIEW? THE DEFERENCE DEBATE IN INTERNATIONAL INVESTMENT LAW

*Johannes Hendrik Fahner**

3.1 INTRODUCTION

In the field of international investment law, foreign investors are commonly granted a right to initiate international arbitration in the case of a dispute with host state authorities. As a consequence, foreign investors can often choose where to lodge a complaint concerning host state action: either in the domestic courts of the host state or before an international arbitral tribunal.[1] When the investor chooses to pursue claims at the international level, an arbitral *ad hoc* tribunal will evaluate the lawfulness of the host state's conduct against treaty standards, such as the fair and equitable treatment standard and the prohibition of expropriation without compensation. It has been noted that, in such circumstances, the tribunal is called upon to fulfil a task similar to that of the administrative or constitutional courts of the host state.[2]

In many municipal legal systems, the judicial review of government conduct is subject to considerations of deference. They are based on the idea that judges do not possess the expertise nor the democratic authorisation to substitute their judgment for that of other governmental authorities. A topical question in the field of international investment law is whether investor-state arbitral tribunals should exercise similar restraint

---

* Many thanks to Başak Bağlayan Ceyhan and Relja Radović for their valuable comments on earlier drafts of this chapter. Many thanks also to Alexander Panayotov for numerous constructive discussions on the topic.
1. The investor's freedom of choice is of course limited by the applicable treaty provisions on waiting periods and fork-in-the-road provisions. See Anne van Aken, 'Primary and Secondary Remedies in International Investment Law and National State Liability. A Functional and Comparative View' in Stephan W Schill (ed), *International Investment Law and Comparative Public Law* (OUP 2010) 739-743. Moreover, the extent to which investors are required to make some effort to obtain local remedies remains controversial. See e.g. George K Foster, 'Striking a Balance between Investor Protections and National Sovereignty: The Relevance of Local Remedies in Investment Treaty Arbitration' (2011) 49 *Columbia Journal of Transnational Law* 2, 201-267; Ursala Kriebaum, 'Local Remedies and the Standards for the Protection of Foreign Investment' in Christina Binder, Ursula Kriebaum, August Reinisch and Stephan Wittich (eds), *International Investment Law for the 21st Century. Essays in Honour of Christoph Schreuer* (OUP 2009) 417-462.
2. Stephan W Schill, 'International Investment Law and Comparative Public Law. An Introduction' in Schill 2010, *supra* note 1, 4; Gus van Harten, *Investment Treaty Arbitration and Public Law* (OUP 2007) 71.

when evaluating the conduct of states. Respondent states have often advocated such an approach, arguing that arbitral tribunals should adopt a non-intrusive standard of review when evaluating government conduct against treaty standards.[3]

Academic calls for deference in investor-state arbitration have been raised in response to growing criticism of the current system.[4] The core of this criticism is that investor-state arbitration subjects government conduct to review by private arbitrators who operate within in a system that favours investor interests over competing public interests. According to a 'Statement of Concern' drafted by a group of scholars in response to the public consultation on the proposed inclusion of investor-state arbitration in the Transatlantic Trade and Investment Partnership (TTIP), investment arbitration 'involves a shift in sovereign priorities toward the interests of foreign owners of major assets and away from those of other actors whose direct representation and participation is limited to democratic processes and judicial institutions'.[5] It has been argued that this type of concern could be resolved by recourse to deferential standards of review. William Burke-White and Andreas von Staden propose that 'the development of new standards of review grounded in comparative public law' can imbue investment treaty arbitration 'with enhanced legitimacy and result in procedures and outcomes broadly acceptable to all stakeholders'.[6] This proposition is not uncontested, however, as various authors have argued that deference is inconsistent with the very purpose of investor-state arbitration.[7]

---

3. E.g. *Glamis Gold, Ltd. v. United States* [2009] UNCITRAL, Award <www.italaw.com/sites/default/files/case-documents/ita0378.pdf> accessed 29 June 2015 [594-595].
4. William Burke-White and Andreas von Staden, 'Private Litigation in a Public Law Sphere: the Standards of Review in Investor-State Arbitrations' (2010) 35 *Yale Journal of International Law* 2, 283-346; William Burke-White and Andreas von Staden, 'The Need for Public Law Standards of Review in Investor-State Arbitrations' in Schill 2010, *supra note* 1, 689-720. See also Erlend M Leonhardsen, 'Treaty Change, Arbitral Practice and the Search for a Balance. Standards of Review and the Margin of Appreciation in International Investment Law' in Lukasz Gruszczynski and Wouter Werner (eds), *Deference in International Courts and Tribunals. Standard of Review and Margin of Appreciation* (OUP 2014) 135-151; Joshua Paine, 'The Project of System-Internal Reform in International Investment Law: An Appraisal' (2015) 6 *Journal of International Dispute Settlement* 2, 345: 'A common diagnosis is that employment of inappropriately strict standards of review has resulted in one fundamental aspect of investment law's legitimacy crisis, namely the impression that tribunals illegitimately intrude into public policy determinations which are properly the responsibility of host state organs'.
5. Peter Muchlinski, Horatia Muir Watt, Gus van Harten, Harm Schepel *et al*, 'Statement of Concern about Planned Provisions on Investment Protection and Investor-State Dispute Settlement (ISDS) in the Transatlantic Trade and Investment Partnership (TTIP)' <www.kent.ac.uk/law/isds_treaty_consultation.html> accessed 29 June 2015. See also José Alvarez, *The Public International Law Regime Governing International Investment* (Hague Academy of International Law 2011) 75-93; Muthucumaraswamy Sornarajah, 'The Case against a Regime on International Investment Law' in Leon E Trakman and Nicola W Ranieri (eds), *Regionalism in International Investment Law* (OUP 2013) 475-498.
6. Burke-White and Von Staden 2010, *supra note* 4, 344-345.
7. Sarah Vasani, 'Bowing to the Queen: Rejecting the Margin of Appreciation Doctrine in International Investment Arbitration' in Ian A Laird and Todd J Weiler (eds), *Investment Treaty Arbitration and*

The current chapter investigates the deference debate in international investment law, outlining the main arguments in favour and against the adoption of deference in investor-state arbitration. It is found that the arguments on both sides depend on broader perspectives on the function of investor-state arbitration and in particular on whether investment protection belongs to the field of public or private law. Once international investment law is understood from a public law perspective and the role of investment tribunals is equated to that of domestic administrative and constitutional courts, the adoption of deference is comprehensible. If, however, international investment law is seen from a private law paradigm and the differences between international arbitration and public law judicial review are emphasised, the adoption of deference becomes more problematic. The current chapter discusses both paradigms in some detail. It is then concluded that different characteristics of the current investment protection regime point in different directions as to its public or private law nature, and that a univocal definition of the 'nature' of international investment law is more normative than empirical. It is also concluded, however, that one of the main assertions of the public law paradigm is misleading, namely that arbitral review should be equalled to the review exercised by domestic administrative and constitutional courts. It is argued here that, unlike domestic judicial review, investment arbitration does not serve to control the exercise of public power within the legal parameters of a constitutional framework. It has a more narrow function, primarily to provide investors with a speedy and international remedy to obtain redress for unforeseen government conduct. Within this context, the logic of deference does not apply in the same manner, because the domestic balance of power between various branches of government is not at risk.

3.2   THE CONCEPT OF DEFERENCE IN DOMESTIC ADJUDICATION

In numerous municipal legal systems, courts accord deference to other branches of government when they review their decisions.[8] It entails a form of respect with regard to the prerogatives and competences of other institutions. More specifically,

---

International Law (Vol 3, JurisNet 2010) 137-169; Kassi D Tallent, 'The Tractor in the Jungle: Why Investment Arbitration Tribunals Should Reject a Margin of Appreciation Doctrine' in Laird and Weiler, Investment Treaty Arbitration and International Law (Vol 3, JurisNet 2010), pp. 111-135. Both authors focus on 'the margin of appreciation', which I understand as an expression of deference. See Jeanrique Fahner, 'The Margin of Appreciation in Investor-State Arbitration: The Prevalence and Desirability of Discretion and Deference' in Nicos Lavranos, Ruth Kok et al (eds), 26 Hague Yearbook of International Law 2013 (2014) 422-495.

8.   See for a comparative account, Susana Galera (ed), Judicial Review. A Comparative Analysis inside the European Legal System (Council of Europe Publishing 2010). Of course, states adhere to different versions and degrees of deference. The distinction between the common law and civil law traditions seems to be of relevance in this regard. See A Stone Sweet and J Matthews, 'Proportionality, Judicial Review, and Global Constitutionalism' in G Bongiovanni, G Sartor and C Valentini (eds), Reasonableness and Law (Springer 2009) 203.

deference implies that the reviewing institution allocates additional weight to the arguments of the institution under review, on grounds unrelated to the merits of the case.[9] It implies a certain limitation of the court's intensity of review.[10] Dependent on the legal issue at stake, this might mean that the court presumes the accuracy of a factual assessment made by a government agency or the fairness of a certain policy adopted by a representative body. The amount of deference granted by the court review increases the likelihood that the conduct under review will be considered lawful.

In legal vocabulary, deference can take various forms. It can be expressed in the form of a relative intensity of scrutiny, such as 'lenient scrutiny' or 'intermediate scrutiny'. Alternatively, deference can be translated into a lenient standard of review, such as reasonableness. The Supreme Court of Canada described this standard in the following way:

> A court conducting a review for reasonableness inquires into the qualities that make a decision reasonable. Reasonableness is concerned mostly with the existence of justification, transparency and intelligibility within the decision-making process and with whether the decision falls within a range of possible, acceptable outcomes which are defensible in respect of the facts and the law. It is a deferential standard which requires respect for the legislative choices to leave some matters in the hands of administrative decision makers.[11]

In the Supreme Court's approach, 'reasonableness' functions as a normative benchmark against which the contested government conduct is being evaluated. Alternative benchmarks pose a negative criterion, such as the standard of 'arbitrary and capricious' found in United States administrative law.[12] It implies that the reviewing court restricts its evaluation to a verification of whether the contested measure was not arbitrary or capricious; once this condition is fulfilled, no further evaluation by the court is required.[13]

---

9. Comp Andrew Legg, *The Margin of Appreciation in International Human Rights Law. Deference and Proportionality* (OUP 2012) 21.
10. Paul Barker, 'Investor-State Arbitration as International Public Law: Deference, Proportionality and the Standard of Review' in Ian A Laird *et al* (eds), *Investment Treaty Arbitration and International Law* (Vol 8, Juris Publishing 2015) 254.
11. *David Dunsmuir v. New Brunswick* [2008] Supreme Court of Canada <http://scc-csc.lexum.com/scc-csc/scc-csc/en/item/2408/index.do> accessed 29 June 2015. See Paul Daly, *A Theory of Deference in Administrative Law: Basis, Application and Scope* (CUP 2012) 15-17.
12. Anna T Katselas, 'Do Investment Treaties Prescribe a Deferential Standard of Review? A Comparative Analysis of the U.S. Administrative Procedure Act's Arbitrary and Capricious Standard of Review and the Fair and Equitable Treatment and Arbitrary or Discriminatory Measures Treaty Standards' (2012) 34 *Michigan Journal of International Law* 1, 87-150.
13. See for a detailed analysis of different forms of deference in investor-state arbitration Esmé Shirlow, 'Deference and Indirect Expropriation Analysis in International Investment Law: Observations on Current Approaches and Frameworks for Future Analysis' (2014) 29 *ICSID Review* 3, 595-626.

Several arguments justify the adoption of deference in domestic public law adjudication. A primary justification is derived from the notion of the separation of powers, which aims to distribute public power among different branches of government in order to prevent an accumulation of power. If courts would engage in an extensive, comprehensive evaluation of decisions made by other governmental institutions, they would effectively substitute their own view for that of the institutions under review. Deference prevents courts from encroaching upon the powers of other branches of government in such a way.

A related argument in favour of deference points out that judicial institutions cannot rely on a direct democratic mandate. It is often argued that the opinion of a small number of unelected judges should not be prioritised over the decisions adopted by institutions that can rely on direct democratic support. This argument depends on how one understands the proper role of judicial review in democratic states. While opponents of judicial review argue that unelected judges should never be empowered to overrule the democratic will, proponents of judicial review argue that democracy is not synonymous with majority rule and that courts have the duty to protect minorities against majorities. Deference allows courts to navigate between these two positions.[14]

In practice, the amount of deference granted by courts will differ depending on the type of decision and institution that is under review.[15] Institutions that rely on a direct democratic mandate may be given more deference than institutions, which lack such legitimation. Likewise, courts may be inclined to adopt a more lenient approach to factual, technical or scientific assessments than to more legal determinations. Given the fact that judges generally do not have expertise in these matters, it is often considered that they should defer to the findings of other, possibly specialised agencies.[16] Another factor that is commonly taken into consideration is the stage of the judicial proceedings. While a first instance court may grant a certain degree of deference to

---

14. See Benedikt Pirker, *Proportionality Analysis and Models of Judicial Review* (Europa Law Publishing 2013) 73-80.
15. Comp *RosInvestCo UK Ltd v. Russia* [2010] SCC V (079/2005) <www.italaw.com/sites/default/files/case-documents/ita0720.pdf> accessed 29 June 2015 [274]: 'one will have to take into account the different functions held by administrative organs and judicial organs of a state and the resulting differences in their discretion when applying the law and in the appeals available against their decisions'.
16. This form of deference has been labelled 'empirical deference', in contrast to 'normative deference' which is granted because of the reasons mentioned earlier. See Caroline Henckels, 'The Role of the Standard of Review and the Importance of Deference in Investor-State Arbitration' in Gruszczynski and Werner (eds) 2014, *supra* note 4, 115-116. See also Lukasz Gruszczynski and Valentina Vadi, 'Standard of Review and Scientific Evidence in WTO Law and International Investment Arbitration. Converging Parallels?' in Gruszczynski and Werner (eds) 2014, *supra* note 4, 152-172; Caroline E Foster, 'Adjudication, Arbitration and the Turn to Public Law 'Standards of Review': Putting the Precautionary Principle in the Crucible' (2012) 3 *Journal of International Dispute Settlement* 3, 525-558; Yuka Fukunaga, 'Standard of Review and "Scientific Truths" in the WTO Dispute Settlement System and Investment Arbitration' (2012) 3 *Journal of International Dispute Settlement* 3, 559-576.

another branch of government, an appeals court normally also attaches weight to the first instance judgment. Arguably, this results in a double degree of deference at the appeals level.[17] Finally, and most importantly, the degree of deference depends on the applicable legal norm against which the contested government act is being reviewed. Courts may consider it relevant to what extent the legal norm is precise and specific and to what extent it leaves discretionary space to the relevant authorities. Whenever courts review compliance with a discretionary norm, they may consider its normative flexibility an additional reason for deference.

3.3   ARGUMENTS IN FAVOUR OF DEFERENCE IN INVESTOR-STATE
            ARBITRATION

Some of the arguments underpinning deference in domestic public law adjudication have been applied in the context of investment arbitration as well. Stephan Schill has argued that since investment tribunals have the same function as domestic courts in public law disputes, tribunals have a sound reason for following their example: 'The domestic court parallel (…) suggests that deference in investment treaty arbitration is justified because domestic courts, when reviewing government conduct, regularly apply a certain degree of deference to implement the idea of the separation of powers'.[18] Similarly, Caroline Henckels has noted that investment arbitration claims 'often involve legal issues that would ordinarily be considered to be constitutional or administrative in nature, and raise the issue of the horizontal dimension of the standard of review in terms of the balance of power between different branches of government'.[19] In addition to the separation of powers, the argument of democratic legitimacy has also been raised in the context of investment arbitration. Henckels notes that 'the adversarial process cannot effectively substitute democratic or other localised decision-making processes'.[20] Similarly, Barnali Choudhury asks: 'if democratically elected governments enact public interest regulations in response to public concerns or to address democratic ideals, how can investment arbitrators make decisions affecting such regulations without public input?'.[21]

---

17. Comp Lukasz Gruszczynski and Wouter Werner, 'Introduction' in Gruszczynski and Werner (eds) 2014, *supra* note 4, 1. See also Dean Spielmann, 'Allowing the Right Margin: The European Court of Human Rights and the National Margin of Appreciation Doctrine: Waiver or Subsidiarity of European Review?' in C Barnard and M Gehring (eds), *Cambridge Yearbook of European Legal Studies* (Vol 14, 2011-2012 Hart 2012) 412-415.

18. Stephan W Schill, 'Deference in Investment Treaty Arbitration: Re-conceptualizing the Standard of Review' (2012) 3 *Journal of International Dispute Settlement* 3, 588.

19. Henckels 2014, *supra* note 16, 121.

20. Caroline Henckels, 'Balancing Investment Protection and the Public Interest: The Role of the Standard of Review and the Importance of Deference in Investor-State Arbitration' (2013) 4 *Journal of International Dispute Settlement* 1, 197-215.

21. Barnali Choudhury, 'Recapturing Public Power: Is Investment Arbitration's Engagement of the Public Interest Contributing to the Democratic Deficit?' (2008) 41 *Vanderbilt Journal of Transnational Law* 3, 779. See also, generally, Andreas von Staden, 'Democratic Legitimacy of Judicial Review beyond the State:

The reasons for granting deference on constitutional and democratic grounds may become more pressing when the issue at stake requires arbitrators to make value judgments on controversial policy questions. Tribunals often insist that they are not requested to review the quality of government decisions in the abstract. The *CMS* tribunal, for example, dealing with claims concerning Argentina's response to the financial crisis of the early 2000s, ruled that its task was not 'to pass judgment on the economic policies adopted by Argentina'.[22] However, when a tribunal is requested to review government conduct against evaluative norms such as the fair and equitable treatment standard, this inevitably involves a degree of value judgment. In such circumstances, it could be argued that arbitral tribunals should defer to the policy choices made by domestic institutions. Indeed, the tribunal in *S.D. Myers v. Canada*, reviewing a Canadian import ban on toxic waste, held that an investment arbitration tribunal:

> does not have an open-ended mandate to second-guess government decision-making. Governments have to make many potentially controversial choices. In doing so, they may appear to have made mistakes, to have misjudged the facts, proceeded on the basis of a misguided economic or sociological theory, placed too much emphasis on some social values over others and adopted solutions that are ultimately ineffective or counterproductive. The ordinary remedy, if there were one, for errors in modern governments is through internal political and legal processes, including elections.[23]

The difficulties involved with reviewing legislation against investment treaty standards have been explicitly addressed by the tribunal in *Paushok v. Mongolia*. The tribunal held that 'actions by legislative assemblies are not beyond the reach of bilateral investment treaties. A State is not immune from claims by foreign investors in connection with legislation passed by its legislative body'.[24] Nonetheless, the tribunal also ruled that 'the fact that a democratically elected legislature has passed legislation that may be considered as ill-conceived, counter-productive and excessively burdensome does not automatically allow to conclude that a breach of an investment treaty has occurred'.[25] This position arguably implies a degree of deference granted to the institutions under review.[26]

Normative Subsidiarity and Judicial Standards of Review' (2012) 10 *International Journal of Constitutional Law* 4, 1023-1049.

22. *CMS Gas Transmission Company v. Argentina* [2005] ICSID Case No ARB/01/8 <www.italaw.com/sites/default/files/case-documents/ita0184.pdf> accessed 1 June 2014 [159].

23. *SD Myers, Inc v. Canada* [2000] UNCITRAL Merits Award <www.italaw.com/sites/default/files/case-documents/ita0747.pdf> accessed 1 June 2014 [261].

24. *Sergei Paushok, CJSC Golden East Company and CJSC Vostokneftegaz Company v. Mongolia* [2011] UNICTRAL, Award on Jurisdiction and Liability <www.italaw.com/sites/default/files/case-documents/ita0622.pdf> accessed 1 June 2014 [298].

25. *Ibid* [299].

26. Jonathan Bonnitcha, *Substantive Protection under Investment Treaties. A Legal and Economic Analysis* (CUP 2014) 213–214: 'The tribunal's view that "ill-conceived, counter-productive and excessively

The *Paushok* tribunal also expressed some sympathy toward the difficult tasks often faced by legislative institutions. The tribunal acknowledged that 'legislative assemblies around the world spend a good part of their time amending substantive portions of existing laws in order to adjust them to changing times or to correct serious mistakes that were made at the time of their adoption'.[27] From this statement, one could deduct another reason for deference, namely that governmental institutions are often required to make difficult decisions in circumstances that are complex but nonetheless demand swift action. Several tribunals have held that arbitrators should not be too critical of such decisions, especially when they could themselves benefit from the benefit of hindsight. For instance, the Annulment Committee reviewing the *Enron v. Argentina* award concerning the Argentine economic crisis wondered whether an assessment of necessity should entail a degree of deference. It questioned whether the credibility of the necessity claim should be determined 'at the date of its award, when the Tribunal may have the benefit of knowledge and hindsight that was not available to the State at the time that it adopted the measure in question'.[28] The Committee appeared to be of the opinion that the tribunal's evaluation should be made 'on the basis of information reasonably available at the time that the measure was adopted' and with regard to the 'margin of appreciation' of the state.[29] In a similar vein, the *Continental Casualty* tribunal accorded a 'significant margin of appreciation' to the respondent state: 'a time of grave crisis is not the time for nice judgments, particularly when examined by others with the disadvantage of hindsight'.[30]

Various authors have argued that while deference is appropriate in the municipal context, it is all the more so in the context of international arbitral review. It has been pointed out that domestic judges are held accountable to the public in various ways, for example through a legislative override. In investment-arbitration, however, there are no comparable accountability mechanisms that tie arbitrators to the public of the host state.[31] On the contrary, it has been argued that arbitrators often lack linkages with the host state's social, political and legal environment. Tribunals are comprised

---

burdensome" legislation would not breach the FET standard clearly precludes substantive review under the FET standard'.

27. *Paushok v. Mongolia, supra* note 24 [299].

28. *Enron Creditors Recovery Corp v. Argentina* [2010] ICSID Case No ARB/01/3, Decision on the Application for Annulment <www.italaw.com/sites/default/files/case-documents/ita0299.pdf> accessed 1 June 2014 [372].

29. *Ibid.*

30. *Continental Casualty Co v. Argentina* [2008] ICSID Case No ARB/03/9, Award <www.italaw.com/sites/default/files/case-documents/ita0228.pdf> accessed 3 June 2014 [181]. See also *Gemplus SA et al and Talsud SA v. Mexico* [2010] ICSID Case No ARB (AF)/04/3 and ARB (AF)/04/4, Award <www.italaw.com/sites/default/files/case-documents/ita0357.pdf> accessed 1 June 2014 [6–26]. The tribunal accorded to the respondent 'a generous margin of appreciation, applied without the benefit of hindsight'.

31. Choudhury 2008, *supra* note 21, 818-819.

of 'non-tenured arbitrators who are not necessarily sufficiently embedded in the social, economic and legal background of a case to undertake an informed balancing exercise'.[32] William Burke-White and Andreas von Staden have argued that, for this reason, arbitrators should defer to assessments made by national authorities: 'lack of embeddedness suggests the need for greater deference to decisions made by institutions that are more culturally, legally, and politically embedded'.[33]

Moreover, it has been argued that international tribunals should be inclined to accord deference to respondent states on grounds of their sovereignty. Although the assumption of obligations under international law is arguably a sovereign act itself that cannot be circumvented on grounds of sovereignty, it could be argued that states are entitled to deference with regard to the interpretation and application of treaty norms. As the masters of the treaty, respondent States can be considered to have the final authority on the interpretation of treaty provisions. Also the idea that State are sovereign as concerns their domestic affairs has been used to defend the desirability of deference. The *S.D. Myers* tribunal famously held that arbitral tribunals should acknowledge 'the high measure of deference that international law generally extends to the right of domestic authorities to regulate matters within their own borders', at least when applying the minimum standard of treatment codified in Article 1105 NAFTA.[34]

Some observers have argued that the concept of deference has become widely accepted by courts and tribunals in diverse fields of international law.[35] Along these lines, the *Continental Casualty* tribunal, referring to the approach of the European Court of Human Rights, held that 'a certain deference' with regard to the application of general standards 'may well be by now a general feature of international law also in respect of the protection of foreign investors under BITs'.[36] This allegedly widespread adoption of deference has been explained with reference to the awareness of courts and tribunals of their limited powers *vis-à-vis* respondent states.[37]

---

32. Pirker 2013, *supra* note 14, 348.
33. Burke-White and Von Staden 2010, *supra* note 6, 332-333.
34. *Myers v. Canada, supra* note 23 [263].
35. Yuval Shany, 'Towards a General Margin of Appreciation Doctrine in International Law?' (2006) 16 *European Journal of International Law* 5, 907-940. Valentina Vadi and Lukasz Gruszczynskzi argue that investment tribunals should follow the example of WTO dispute settlement bodies concerning deference. Valentina Vadi and Lukasz Gruszczynskzi, 'Standards of Review in International Investment Law and Arbitration: Multilevel Governance and the Commonweal' (2013) 16 *Journal of International Economic Law* 3, 613–633.
36. *Continental Casualty v. Argentina, supra* note 30 [footnote 270].
37. Leonhardsen 2014, *supra* note 4, 139: deference is 'a rational response to the problem of institutional weakness that characterises international courts and tribunals in times when (...) States and those who influence States voice strong criticism'.

With regard to deference in the context of factual and scientific determinations, it has been noted that arbitral tribunals normally lack the expertise to second-guess determinations made by domestic agencies. Unlike domestic institutions, tribunals are not supported by bureaucracies or specialised agencies that can compete with those of respondent states. For this reason, national authorities arguably deserve a degree of deference. As noted by Stephan Schill, the expertise of domestic authorities may 'speak in favour of respecting factual determinations made by domestic institutions, rather than supporting full-blown review by investment treaty tribunals' and of 'respecting science-based determinations made by domestic agencies'.[38] In the case of *Glamis Gold v. United States*, the respondent state raised exactly this argument: 'a high measure of deference to the facts and factual conclusions seems the only way to prevent investment tribunals from becoming science courts'.[39]

A circumstantial argument for deference applies once the contested government act has already been reviewed by domestic courts. If an investor brings an investment treaty claim after domestic remedies have been pursued, this usually means that the tribunal has to rule on the same matter as domestic courts before it.[40] In this situation, the tribunal may consider that the contested government act has already been reviewed by a presumably independent judicial institution before the treaty claim was brought, which arguably implies a ground for deference. However, investors may also complain that the manner in which domestic courts applied domestic law constituted a violation of treaty rights in itself, for example under the fair and equitable treatment standard or under a claim for denial of justice. This requires the tribunal to review the domestic courts' application of domestic law. As tribunals have often acknowledged, however, they are not meant to operate as courts of appeal, while domestic courts may be presumed to know the domestic law of their legal system, at least more so than international arbitral tribunals. This presumption is arguably a strong ground for deference whenever tribunals are required to review the domestic courts' application of municipal law.

3.4   ARGUMENTS AGAINST DEFERENCE IN INVESTOR-STATE
           ARBITRATION

In response to the various argument raised by academic observers and respondent states in favour of deference, opponents have brought up various reasons that militate against the adoption of deference. On a general level, it has been emphasised that by

---

38. Schill 2012, *supra* note 18, 602.
39. *Glamis Gold v. United States*, *supra* note 3 [594].
40. Treaty standards often provide similar protection as municipal standards: 'the protective provisions in international investment agreements (IIAs) cover grounds similar to that covered by administrative law or state liability law in municipal orders'. Van Aken 2010, *supra* note 1, 721.

adopting arbitration clauses in investment treaties, states have themselves empowered arbitral tribunals to interpret and apply treaty norms. As noted by the Renta 4 tribunal, 'when agreeing to the jurisdiction of international tribunals, states perforce accept that those jurisdictions will exercise their judgment'.[41] In a similar vein, the *Enron* tribunal held:

> Judicial determination of the compliance with the requirements of international law in this matter should not be understood as if arbitral tribunals might be wishing to substitute for the functions of the sovereign State, but simply responds to the duty that in applying international law they cannot fail to give effect to legal commitments that are binding on the parties and interpret the rules accordingly.[42]

Admittedly, the mandate given to tribunals to settle disputes between states and investors does not yet tell them how to exercise their review. It could be argued, however, that deference constitutes a constraint of this mandate, which should be explicitly ordered by the relevant treaty.[43]

More specific objections against deference relate to the reasons which compelled states to grant foreign investors access to international arbitration. It should be noted that investment arbitration provides investors with a unique remedy to challenge host state conduct as an alternative to domestic courts. The ICSID Convention itself acknowledges that investment disputes are normally capable of being settled through domestic proceedings.[44] This raises the question of why states offer international arbitration as an alternative to domestic court litigation.[45] A common answer to this question points to the vulnerable position of the foreign investor in the environment of the host state. As noted by Thomas Wälde in his Separate Opinion to the *Thunderbird*

41. *Quasar de Valores SICAV SA, Orgor de Valores SICAV SA, GBI 9000 SICAV SA, ALOS 34 SL (Renta 4) v. Russia* [2012] SCC V (024/2007) Award <www.italaw.com/sites/default/files/case-documents/ ita1075.pdf> accessed 1 June 2014 [179]. The award is commonly named after the first original claimant that was denied standing by the tribunal in preliminary award.

42. *Enron Corp and Ponderosa Assets, LP v. Argentina* [2007] ICSID Case No ARB/01/3 <www.italaw.com/ sites/default/files/case-documents/ita0293.pdf> accessed 1 June 2014 [340].

43. James Egerton-Vernon, 'Is Investment Treaty Arbitration a Mechanism to Second-Guess Government's Exercise of Administrative Discretion: Public Law or *Lex Investoria*' in Laird *et al* (eds) 2010, *supra* note 10, 201-233; Paine 2015, *supra* note 4, 346.

44. ICSID Convention Preamble: '(…) Bearing in mind the possibility that from time to time disputes may arise in connection with such investment between Contracting States and nationals of other Contracting States; Recognizing that while such disputes would usually be subject to national legal processes, international methods of settlement may be appropriate in certain cases (…)'.

45. See Leon E Trakman, 'Australia's Rejection of Investor-State Arbitration: A Sign of Global Change' in Leon E Trakman and Nicola W Ranieri (eds), *Regionalism in International Investment Law* (OUP 2013) 356-362; Christoph Schreuer, 'Do We Need Investment Arbitration?' in Jean E Kalicki and Anna Joubin-Bret (eds), *Reshaping the Investor-State Dispute Settlement System. Journeys for the 21st Century* (Brill 2015) 879-889.

Award, this position is frequently one of 'structural weakness', because the investor is subjected to the host state's regulatory, administrative and judicial powers.[46] Admittedly, this hierarchical relationship applies to domestic investors as well, but there are certain aspects of the foreign investor's position that may render his situation worse. Firstly, a foreign investor may fear that domestic institutions are biased against him because of his foreign nationality. Secondly, even when such bias is absent, foreign investor may be at a disadvantage in the municipal legal order, because the legal, social, political and cultural environment of the host state is alien to him.[47] When states adopt arbitration clauses in investment treaties, they seek to rebalance the investor's position by offering him access to an international, neutral forum unrelated to the host state itself.

Individuals or corporations engaging in foreign investment enter the situation of 'structural weakness' described by Wälde of their own free will. When the Australian government renounced the practice of investor-state arbitration, it concluded: 'If Australian businesses are concerned about sovereign risk in Australian trading partner countries, they will need to make their own assessments about whether they want to commit to investing in those countries'.[48] It should be noted, however, that states who provide international investment protection do so because they want to attract foreign investment. When states offer potential investors the right to initiate international arbitration, they intend to enhance their credibility and attractiveness as host state.[49] The right to initiate arbitration is supposed to sooth investor concerns over political risk, because potential arbitration claims might prevent the host state from adopting unlawful measures or at least because the arbitration process might provide the investor with compensation in case the preventive effect would fail.

If understood in this way, the purpose of investor-state arbitration could be considered antagonistic to the concept of deference. Access to international arbitration

---

46. *International Thunderbird Gaming Corporation v. Mexico* [2005] UNCITRAL, Separate Opinion of Thomas Wälde <www.italaw.com/sites/default/files/case-documents/ita0432.pdf> accessed 31 October 2014 [12].
47. Thomas Wälde, 'The Specific Nature of Investment Arbitration' in P Kahn and T Wälde (eds), *New Aspects of International Investment Law* (Martinus Nijhoff 2007) 54-55.
48. Australian Government Department of Foreign Affairs and Trade, 'Gillard Government Trade Policy Statement: Trading our Way to More Jobs and Prosperity' (2011) <www.acci.asn.au/getattachment/b9d3cfae-fc0c-4c2a-a3df-3f58228daf6d/Gillard-Government-Trade-Policy-Statement.aspx> accessed 31 October 2014.
49. See Jeswald W Salacuse and Nicholas P Sullivan, 'Do BITs Really Work? An Evaluation of Bilateral Investment Treaties and Their Grand Bargain' (2005) 46 *Harvard International Law Journal* 1, 67-130, describing the conclusion of investment treaties between capital-exporting and capital-importing states as a 'grand bargain: a *promise* of protection of capital in return for the *prospect* of more capital in the future'. Some authors have described the development of the BIT network in more critical terms. See e.g. Kate Miles, *The Origins of International Investment Law: Empire, Environment and the Safeguarding of Capital* (CUP 2013).

enables investors to bring complaints in a dispute settlement forum that is unrelated to the host state. As noted by Kassi Tallent, 'the assurance that the investor may have his or her case decided by an impartial, international tribunal is probably the most important promise offered by the state in exchange for the expected benefit of foreign investment'.[50] The logic of deference does not fit with this rationale behind investor-state arbitration. Deference implies that the power to interpret treaty requirements is being shifted back to the host state authorities. By granting deference to the respondent state, tribunals weaken the independent nature of their review. For the same reasons, the alleged lack of embeddedness in the social, economic and cultural background of the host state which distinguishes arbitrators from domestic judges and which has been lamented by Burke-White and von Staden cannot be considered problematic. On the contrary, the lack of ties to the host state is precisely the reason why arbitrators are chosen to review a dispute.

Investment arbitration does not only aspire to be independent, but it also assumes that the parties involved are equal before the tribunal. Sarah Vasani argues that 'a fundamental principle of the investment arbitration system irrespective of the fact that sovereign States are involved is that both parties are to be treated equally'.[51] Deference, however, accords extra weight to the views of one of the parties, namely the host state. By adopting considerations of deference like those common in domestic courts, investment tribunals would reintroduce the inequality between the parties that was a main reason for establishing the arbitration system in the first place.[52]

Arguments related to the normative openness of investment treaty standards have been raised on both sides of the debate. On the one hand, it has been argued that respondent states are entitled to deference, because common investment treaty standards are open-ended and leave a wide discretionary space to host state authorities.[53] On the other hand, it has been observed that since treaty standards pose only minimum obligations for host states, the review exercised by tribunals is already of a very limited nature, which reduces the need for further deference. This is the approach

---

50. Tallent, 'The Tractor in the Jungle', *supra* note 7, 130. See also *Gas Natural SDG v. Argentina* [2005] ICSID Case No ARB/03/10 [29]: 'assurance of independent international arbitration is an important – perhaps the most important – element in investor protection'.
51. Vasani 2010, *supra* note 7, 164.
52. Moreover, it has been argued that in practice the state always enjoys advantages over the investor. For instance, the state has various ways of interfering with arbitration cases that the investor lacks. Charles N Brower, 'W(h)ither International Commercial Arbitration. The Goff Lecture 2007' (2008) 24 *Arbitration International: The Journal of LCIA Worldwide Arbitration* 2, 189-190. This argument renders deference even more undesirable. See also Thomas W. Wälde, 'Procedural Challenges in Investment Arbitration under the Shadow of the Dual Role of the State: Asymmetries and Tribunals' Duty to Ensure, Pro-actively, the Equality of Arms' (2010) 26 *Arbitration International* 1, 3-42.
53. See Anne van Aken, 'International Investment Law between Commitment and Flexibility: A Contract Theory Analysis' (2009) 12 *Journal of International Economic Law* 2, 527-531.

taken by the *Glamis Gold* tribunal. It disagreed with the respondent 'that domestic deference in national court systems is necessarily applicable to international tribunals'.[54] The tribunal found 'the standard of deference to already be present in the standard as stated, rather than being additive to that standard', because a breach of Article 1105 NAFTA required 'something greater than mere arbitrariness, something that is surprising, shocking, or exhibits a manifest lack of reasoning'.[55] The reasoning of the *Glamis Gold* tribunal shows the complexities of the relationship between deference and the flexibility of the applicable norm. While some observers argue that a flexible norm is a reason for granting deference, the *Glamis Gold* approach implies that since the applicable norm is already lenient, there is no need for 'additional' deference.[56]

Specific arguments have been raised against deference on grounds of the separation of powers and the democratic legitimacy of host state measures. It has been pointed out that in various host states, democratic modes of decision-making are absent and administrative agencies lack expertise or suffer from corruption. In those circumstances, the logic of the separation of powers becomes problematic. Moreover, even when domestic decision-making procedures reflect the popular will, this may have less relevance in the context of international investment law than in the domestic constitutional scheme. Investment treaty protection may actually be offered precisely to protect foreign investors from the popular will in certain circumstances, since foreign investments are common targets of domestic discontent, especially in times of economic crisis.[57]

Furthermore, it has been emphasised that foreign investors do not participate in domestic decision-making processes. Domestic public law courts grant deference to other branches of government in order to respect the democratic will and also because discontented citizens have other means to advance their cause, such as their vote. Foreign investors do not have the same position. As noted by Kassi Tallent, 'the investor is an outsider to the democratic processes influencing the development and application of state regulatory measures'.[58] The *Tecmed* tribunal, reviewing the closing of an industrial waste landfill, expressed the same rationale:

> the foreign investor has a reduced or nil participation in the taking of the decisions that affect it, partly because the investors are not entitle to exercise political rights reserved to the

---

54. *Glamis Gold v. United States, supra* note 3 [617].
55. *Ibid.*
56. See for the same argument Rahim Moloo and Justin M Jacinto, 'Standards of Review and Reviewing Standards: Public Interest Regulation in International Investment Law' in Karl P Sauvant (ed), *Yearbook on International Investment Law and Policy 2011-2012* (OUP 2013) 539-567.
57. Anthea Roberts, 'Clash of Paradigms: Actors and Analogies Shaping the Investment Treaty System' (2013) 107 *American Journal of International Law* 1, 68; Vasani 2010, *supra* note 7, 167. M Sornarajah, *The International Law on Foreign Investment* (3rd edn, CUP 2010) 71-72.
58. Tallent, 'The Tractor in the Jungle', *supra* note 7, 130.

nationals of the State, such as voting for the authorities that will issue the decisions that affect such investors.[59]

The investor's exclusion from domestic politics arguably militates against the adoption of domestic concepts such as the separation of powers within the context of investment law. Within the domestic scheme, judicial deference expresses respect towards the decisions taken by other institutions with democratic involvement. Because foreign investors are not similarly involved in domestic decision-making procedures, the logic of deference cannot be applied in the same way in investor-state arbitration.

Various tribunals have rejected the argument that deference has become a general feature of international adjudication. When the respondent in *Siemens v. Argentina* invoked the case law of the European Court of Human Rights, the tribunal held that this Court applied a 'margin of appreciation not found in customary international law'.[60] The *Renta 4* tribunal also objected to the idea that the concept of the 'margin of appreciation' should be applied in the context of investment law. Comparing the protection offered by a BIT to the protection offered by human rights treaties, the tribunal held:

> Human rights conventions establish minimum standards to which all individuals are entitled irrespective of any act of volition on their part, whereas investment-protection treaties contain undertakings which are explicitly designed to induce foreigners to make investments in reliance upon them. It therefore makes sense that the reliability of an instrument of the latter kind should not be diluted by precisely the same notions of 'margins of appreciation' that apply to the former.[61]

According to the tribunal, the purpose of human rights protection on the one hand and investment protection on the other hand is too different to allow a cross-regime application of the margin of appreciation.

In general, it appears that tribunals are reluctant to accord deference to the determinations made by respondent states. On the basis of an investigation of 243 investment arbitration awards, Gus van Harten has concluded that arbitrators are more likely to engage in unrestrained review than domestic courts. According to van Harten, tribunals 'assumed far-reaching authority to oversee states intensively in relation to legislative and executive decision-making and in spite of the overlapping role of other

---

59. *Técnicas Medioambientales Tecmed SA v. Mexico* (2003) ICSID Case No ARB (AF)/00/2 <www.italaw. com/sites/default/files/case-documents/ita0854.pdf> accessed 15 September 2015 [122].

60. *Siemens AG v. Argentina* (2007) ICSID Case No ARB/02/8 <www.italaw.com/sites/default/files/case-documents/ita0790.pdf> accessed 15 September 2015 [354].

61. *Renta 4 v. Russia, supra* note 41 [22].

adjudicators'.[62] He concludes that the current tendency among arbitrators is 'to assert explicitly or implicitly an expansive role for themselves to decide whether the choices and conduct of another decision-maker were correct'.[63]

3.5   THE FUNCTION OF INVESTOR-STATE ARBITRATION: PRIVATE LAW
           DISPUTE SETTLEMENT OR PUBLIC LAW JUDICIAL REVIEW?

The ultimate answer to the question of whether investment tribunals should defer to domestic authorities seems to be related to broader perspectives on the nature or character of investor-state arbitration. In particular, it appears that the concept of deference is more widely appreciated by observers who emphasise the public law characteristics of investor-state arbitration, while observers familiar with a private law perspective are more critical of its adoption.[64]

It has often been pointed out that investor-state arbitration is modelled after commercial arbitration.[65] International commercial arbitration, developed in order to provide parties in cross-border business disputes with a speedy and presumably neutral adjudication mechanism, has several features which states consider useful for the settlement of investment disputes as well. Compared with court adjudication, arbitration is hailed for its speediness, neutrality and the possible confidentiality of the proceedings. States endorse commercial arbitration out of respect for 'the autonomous decisions of commercial actors to displace the courts' competence and replace it with a mutually constructed alternative'.[66]

Investor-state arbitration shares many of the procedural characteristics of commercial arbitration.[67] In both types of proceedings, disputing parties agree to bring their dispute before an *ad hoc* tribunal, of which all or some of the members are chosen by the

---

62. Gus van Harten, *Sovereign Choices and Sovereign Constraints: Judicial Restraint in Investment Treaty Arbitration* (OUP 2013) 17. See also Gus van Harten, 'Judicial Restraint in Investment Treaty Arbitration: Restraint Based on Relative Suitability' (2014) 5 *Journal of International Dispute Settlement* 1, 5-39.

63. *Ibid* 162. This does of course not necessarily mean that the state is found in breach. See Susan D Franck, 'Empirically Evaluating Claims about Investment Treaty Arbitration', 86 *North Carolina Law Review* 1 (2007) 84, finding 'reasonably equivalent investor and state win rates'.

64. Anthea Roberts, 'The Next Battleground: Standards of Review in Investment Treaty Arbitration' (2011) *International Council for Commercial Arbitration Congress Series No 16* (2011) 170-180; Julian Arato, 'The Margin of Appreciation in International Investment Law' (2014) 54 *Virginia Journal of International Law* 3, 555; Egerton-Vernon 2010, *supra* note 43, 201-233.

65. Barton Legum, 'Investment Treaty Arbitration's Contribution to International Commercial Arbitration – The Effects of Investment Treaty Arbitration on International Commercial Arbitration, and their Significance' (2005) 60 *Dispute Resolution Journal* 3, 70-75.

66. Van Harten 2007, *supra* note 2, 61.

67. For some differences, see Karl-Heinz Böckstiegel, 'Commercial and Investment Arbitration: How Different Are They Today? The Lalive Lecture 2012' (2012) 28 *Arbitration International* 4, 577-590.

parties. The tribunal is empowered to rule on its own jurisdiction and the outcome of the proceedings is a damage award that is binding on the parties. The isolation from court review that characterises commercial arbitration occurs in investor-state arbitration as well, since investor-state awards cannot be set aside by domestic courts, except in cases of serious procedural shortcomings.[68]

The private law origins of investor-state arbitration are widely acknowledged. Moreover, some authors argue that the type of obligations at stake in international investment law are of a private nature. Moshe Hirsch, for example, contends that 'international investment law emphasises the private law aspects of the relations between host governments and foreign investors'.[69] According to Hirsch, the primary inquiry undertaken in the context of investment arbitration focuses on obligations deriving from promises made by state authorities and from the regulatory framework as it existed when the investment was negotiated and entered into. For this reason, Hirsch argues, international investment law 'largely aims to protect various private law undertakings that are made between the host state and the foreign investor'.[70] From this perspective, investment arbitration does not serve to evaluate the lawfulness of government in the abstract, but only to verify whether the assurances relied on by the investor were complied with.

In spite of the private law roots of international arbitration, observers have started to stress the public law characteristics of international investment law.[71] A first element that has been emphasised in this regard is the source of the consent to arbitration on the side of the state. Historically, most arbitrations between a state and a foreign investor depended on arbitration clauses provided in investment contracts.[72] The main innovation of the current international investment law regime was the codification of general consent to arbitration in investment protection treaties.[73] As a result of this general consent, any party who fell within the definitions of the treaty became

---

68. Lars Markert and Helene Bubrowski, 'National Setting Aside Proceedings in Investment Arbitration' in Marc Bungenberg *et al* (eds), *International Investment Law. A Handbook* (Hart 2015) 1460-1481.
69. Moshe Hirsch, 'Investment Tribunals and Human Rights: Divergent Paths' in Pierre-Marie Dupuy, Ernst-Ulrich Petersmann and Francesco Francioni, *Human Rights in International Investment Law and Arbitration* (OUP 2009) 114.
70. *Ibid* 109.
71. Gus van Harten and Martin Loughlin, 'Investment Treaty Arbitration as a Species of Global Administrative Law' (2006) 17 *European Journal of International Law* 1, 121-150; Santiago Montt, *State Liability in Investment Treaty Arbitration* (Hart 2009); Stephan W Schill, 'Enhancing International Investment Law's Legitimacy: Conceptual and Methodological Foundations of a New Public Law Approach' (2011) 52 *Virginia Journal of International Law* 1 (2011) 57-102. See also Barry Leon and John Terry, 'Special Considerations When a State is a Party to International Arbitration. Why Arbitrating against a State is Different: 12 Key Reasons' (2006) 61 *Dispute Resolution Journal* 1, 68-76.
72. Van Harten 2007, *supra* note 2, 63.
73. See Surya P Subedi, *International Investment Law. Reconciling Policy and Principle* (Hart 2008) 32-33, speaking about a 'silent revolution in foreign investment law'.

entitled to initiate an arbitration claim. According to van Harten, this innovation transformed 'international arbitration from a form of reciprocally consensual adjudication into a governing arrangement'.[74] General consent to arbitration has created a new layer of arbitral control of government conduct.

A second characteristic of the current international investment law regime, which is emphasised in the public law paradigm is the subject matter of common investment disputes. It has been argued that these disputes are not limited to contractual disputes concerning the state's private conduct, but instead involve its exercise of public power and potentially affect entire populations.[75] As noted by Stephan Schill, investment arbitration disputes often concern domestic policy-making, as is evident from cases concerning water concessions, affirmative action programs, environmental protection measures, public health programs and economic reforms.[76] In a similar vein, Burke-White and von Staden note that investment arbitration is not restricted to 'merely technical questions', but 'frequently implicates the scope of the regulatory powers of the respondent state'.[77] Consequently, investment arbitration engages with contested policy choices, with the balancing of private and public interests and with the state's general definition of the public good. These issues are commonly considered to fall within the scope of public law. A related argument concerns the relationship between the different parties involved. Investment treaties are signed between equal, sovereign states and disputing parties are considered equal before arbitral tribunals. In their everyday relationship, however, the relationship between the disputing parties is one between sovereign and subordinate. The law that governs this sort of relationship is typically considered public law.

A third characteristic of international investment law that allegedly demonstrates its public law nature is the contribution of investment arbitration awards to the development of international law. Stephan Schill has argued that international investment law is not only concerned with 'backing up private ordering between foreign investors and host states', but instead with 'providing a legal framework for a public international economic order'.[78] While investment arbitration awards do not formally have the value of precedent, in reality awards are often quoted and discussed by subsequent tribunals ruling on similar matters. This is not surprising given the fact that different cases often concern similarly phrased treaty provisions or standards of customary international law. Consequently, although no formal rule of precedent exists

---

74. Van Harten 2007, *supra* note 2, 64.
75. Barker 2015, *supra* note 10, 238: 'The central premise of this paper is that investor-state arbitration can directly affect the lives of entire populations who are not parties to, and are far removed from, any particular case'.
76. Schill 2012, *supra* note 18, 577-578.
77. Burke-White and Von Staden 2010, *supra* note 4, 284.
78. Schill 2010, *supra* note 2, 3.

in international investment law, in reality awards have an impact that goes beyond the specific case at hand.[79]

In conjunction with the adoption of a public law paradigm in international investment law, observes have started to define the function of investment arbitration in terms of 'judicial review'.[80] Federico Ortino, for example, has argued that 'the main object of an investment treaty is the establishment of a system of judicial review reserved for foreign investors'.[81] Similarly, Stephan Schill has proposed that investor-state arbitration should be viewed as 'more akin to administrative or constitutional judicial review than to commercial arbitration'.[82] Arbitration allows the investor, as a subordinate of the state, to challenge government action. Within the domestic scheme, such challenges are normally dealt with by domestic courts who are empowered to engage in administrative or constitutional judicial review. Gus van Harten summarised the point as follows:

> In many states, adjudication plays an important and expanding role in regulating relations between individuals and the state. One of the core functions of the judiciary is to constrain the exercise of sovereign authority by executive government and, under many constitutions, by the legislature. When a judge invokes his or her public law competence to resolve a dispute between the state and a person or organization that is subject to regulation by the state, he or she determines matters such as the legality of governmental activity, the degree to which individuals should be protected from regulation, and the appropriate role of the state. The role of arbitrators under investment treaties is essentially the same.[83]

The public law paradigm in international investment law seems to have found wide acceptance in academia. This has clear consequences for the debate on deference. Once investor-state arbitration is understood as a judicial review mechanism in a public law field, the case for deference becomes much stronger, while the arguments against deference are sometimes being rejected as an obsolete insistence on the private law origins of international arbitration.[84]

---

79. Comp *Saipem S.p.A. v. Bangladesh* (2009) ICSID Case No ARB/07/7 <www.italaw.com/sites/default/ files/case-documents/ita0734.pdf> accessed 15 September 2015 [90]: 'The Tribunal considers that it is not bound by previous decisions. At the same time, it is of the opinion that it must pay due consideration to earlier decisions of international tribunals. It believes that, subject to compelling contrary grounds, it has a duty to adopt solutions established in a series of consistent cases. It also believes that, subject to the specifics of a given treaty and of the circumstances of the actual case, it has a duty to seek to contribute to the harmonious development of investment law and thereby to meet the legitimate expectations of the community of States and investors towards certainty of the rule of law'.
80. See e.g. *International Thunderbird v. Mexico*, Opinion Thomas Wälde, supra note 46 [13].
81. Federico Ortino, 'The Investment Treaty System as Judicial Review' (2013) 24 *American Review of International Arbitration* 3, 443.
82. Schill 2010, *supra* note 2, 4.
83. Van Harten 2007, *supra* note 2, 71.
84. Other issues to which the distinction matters are e.g., transparency, third-party participation and the relevance of norms originating from other fields of international law, such as human rights or

It should be noted, however, that the public law paradigm in international investment law is not without weaknesses. For instance, it leaves unclear why states opted for the mechanism of arbitration in the first place. As noted by Anthea Roberts, 'public law proponents assume that the choice of arbitration was not intended to import private law concepts or approaches into the field, or that, if it were, this was a mistake that should be rectified by the introduction of an international investment court'.[85] Instead, it could be argued that states deliberately chose for international arbitration, because they wanted the international remedy reserved for foreign investors to have a more narrow function than public law adjudication.[86]

In sum, it appears that some characteristics of investor-state arbitration seem to demonstrate its public law nature, while other characteristics fit better in a private law paradigm.[87] Arguably, investment law 'is not a subgenre of an existing discipline. It is dramatically different from anything previously known in the international sphere'.[88] Consequently, discussions on whether the public law or the private law paradigm provide the best conceptual framework for understanding investor-state arbitration cannot be concluded on the basis of empirical arguments alone. Since the system comprises both public and private law characteristics, observers will emphasise the relevance of those elements that fit with their normative assumptions.[89]

Nonetheless, it is concluded here that some of the public law arguments are misleading, notably the idea that investment arbitration is a form of judicial review. In spite of the similarities between investment arbitration and municipal administrative and constitutional adjudication, it appears that the purpose of both types of proceedings is fundamentally different. It seems that while the purpose of domestic court

---

environmental law. Roberts 2013, *supra* note 57, 65. Answers to questions related to consistency and precedent may also depend on the chosen paradigm. See Susan D Franck, 'The Legitimacy Crisis in Investment Treaty Arbitration: Privatizing Public International Law through Inconsistent Decisions', 73 *Fordham Law Review* 1521 (2004-2005). See also Benedict Kingsbury and Stephan W Schill, 'Public Law Concepts to Balance Investors' Rights with the State Regulatory Actions in the Public Interest – the Concept of Proportionality' in Schill 2010, supra note 1, 75-104.

85. Roberts 2013, *supra* note 57, 68.
86. Katselas 2012, *supra* note 12, 147: 'the use of arbitration rather than adjudication is meaningful and suggests that states may have had a dispute-settlement rather than an administrative review function in mind when they signed onto the system'; Egerton-Vernon 2010, *supra* note 43, 231: investor-state arbitration 'was deliberately designed by States to be a hybrid system, a *lex investoria* incorporating a private international arbitration model designed to address disputes that often involve issues of public international law'.
87. Stephan Wittich, 'State Responsiblity' in Bungenberg 2015, *supra* note 68, 37, noting the 'hybrid nature of investment law'.
88. Jan Paulsson, 'Arbitration without Privity' (1995), 10 *ICSID Review* 2, 232. Quoted in Roberts 2013, *supra* note 57, 94.
89. See for a general argument against the distinction between public and private international law Alex Mills, *The Confluence of Public and Private International Law. Justice, Pluralism and Subsidiarity in the International Constitutional Ordering of Private Law* (CUP 2009).

adjudication is to ensure the legitimacy of the exercise of public power, the purpose of investment arbitration is only to compensate foreign investors for damages that, if foreseen, would have prevented them from investing.

The narrow purpose of investment arbitration in comparison to domestic court adjudication can be demonstrated with reference to the remedies available in both types of proceedings. As noted by Anne van Aken, it is helpful to distinguish between primary remedies, which have a preventive or restorative function and include declaratory actions and injunctions, and secondary remedies, which are directed at pecuniary damages. Van Aken contends: 'whereas municipal legal orders tend to be reluctant to grant pecuniary damages and require the use of (preventive) primary remedies against the (illegal) act *per se*, international investment law most heavily relies on *ex post* secondary remedies'.[90] A similar point is raised by Andreas Kulick, who argues that in domestic courts the greatest concern of the state is to avoid 'the stigma of unlawfulness'. In investor-state arbitration, on the other hand, the host state is mostly concerned with avoiding liability, according to Kulick.[91] Of course, arbitral tribunals cannot award compensation without the finding of a treaty violation, while plaintiffs in domestic courts often also seek monetary compensation for unlawful government conduct. This does not mean, however, that the primary purpose of both mechanisms is similar. Compensation appears to be the core aim of investment arbitration, while public law adjudication has a broader role in ensuring the legitimacy of public governance. As noted by José Alvarez, the purpose of investor-state dispute settlement is not to force states to correct their mistakes, but 'to secure a compensatory remedy for past harms done'.[92]

In theory, investment tribunals have the formal power to order other remedies than compensation, but in reality this rarely occurs, for several reasons.[93] Firstly, by definition an investor-state arbitration claim is related to an investment, so the ultimate interest of the applicant is probably a monetary interest. Moreover, investment arbitration claims are mostly raised once the investment has already been terminated and the investor's interests have been reduced to obtaining compensation. Secondly, the enforcement of secondary remedies is more feasible than that of primary remedies granted at the international level. A pecuniary award is enforceable through domestic

---

90. Van Aken 2010, *supra* note 1, 723.
91. Andreas Kulick, 'Book Review' of Schill, *supra* note 1 (2011) 22 *European Journal of International Law* 3, 922.
92. Alvarez 2011, *supra* note 5, 52.
93. Pirker 2013, *supra* note 14, 347; Christoph Schreuer, 'Non-Pecuniary Remedies in ICSID Arbitration' (2004) 20 *Arbitration International* 4, 325-332; Berk Demirkol, 'Remedies in Investment Treaty Arbitration' (2015) 6 *Journal of International Dispute Settlement* 2, 403-426. See for an argument in favour of non-pecuniary remedies Gisele Stephens-Chu, 'Is it Always All About the Money? The Appropriateness of Non-Pecuniary Remedies in Investment Treaty Arbitration' (2014) 30 *Arbitration International* 4, 661-686.

courts on grounds of the ICSID Convention or the New York Convention, while a primary remedy requires more readiness to cooperate on the side of the state.[94] Some tribunals have explicitly refused to order other remedies than compensation. The tribunal in *LG&E v. Argentina*, for example, held that it was not empowered to order a 'modification of the current legal situation by annulling or enacting legislative and administrative measures'.[95] This would imply an 'undue interference' with the respondent's sovereignty'.[96] Because tribunals are reluctant to engage in such interference, investment awards have normally no impact on the domestic legitimacy of the contested measure. This distinguishes awards from domestic court judgments, which can result in the nullification or invalidation of legislation or administrative measures.

It has been argued that even when arbitral tribunals order only monetary awards, the sheer amount of compensation may have serious consequences for the host state. A famous example is the case of *CME v. Czech Republic*. According to Van Harten, 'the award of $353 million placed an enormous strain on the public finances of the Czech Republic', equalling the country's entire health-care budget.[97] Financial burdens of this kind may effectively force the host state to change its policies, for example when there is a risk of further claims by other investors in similar circumstances.[98] In general, however, it seems that tribunals do not often order large amounts of compensation. Investors commonly obtain only a fraction of the amounts claimed, if anything at all. Of a total number of 82 cases analysed by Susan Franck in 2007, only 22 resulted in a damage award and only in 4 cases the tribunals awarded more than $10 million.[99] On the basis of this analysis, Franck suggests that the average amount of damages awarded by investor-state arbitration tribunals is comparable to those granted by other international adjudicators.[100] Moreover, even when tribunals award damages, host states have various means to resist enforcement and prevent the investor from recovering their money. Consequently, it seems that although awards in theory have the potential to substantially affect host state policies, in reality this may hardly ever happen.

---

94.   Van Aken 2010, *supra* note 1, 734. See also Article 54(1) ICSID Convention. Stephan Wittich, 'Investment Arbitration: Remedies' in Bungenberg 2015, *supra* note 68, 1401-1402.
95.   *LG&E Energy Corp v. Argentina* [2007] ICSID Case No ARB/02/1, Award <www.italaw.com/documents/LGEEnglish.pdf> accessed 1 July 2015 [87]. See, critically, Wittich 2015, *supra* note 94, 1398-1400.
96.   *LG&E v. Argentina, supra* note 95 [87]. But see Thomas W Walde and Borzu Sabahi, 'Compensation, Damages, and Valuation' in Peter Muchlinski *et al* (eds), *The Oxford Handbook of International Investment Law* (OUP 2008) 1055-1056, pointing out that an order to re-do a procedurally flawed decision may be less intrusive than a large damages award.
97.   *CME Czech Republic BV v. Czech Republic* [2003] UNCITRAL, Final Award <www.italaw.com/sites/default/files/case-documents/ita0180.pdf> accessed 15 September 2015; Van Harten 2007, *supra* note 2, 7.
98.   Choudhury 2008, *supra* note 21, footnote 319.
99.   Franck 2007, *supra* note 63, 55-66.
100. *Ibid* 58.

The review exercised by domestic administrative and constitutional courts forms part of the checks and balances that have been developed within systems of government in order to prevent powerful actors to seize public power at the cost of other actors and to prevent a tyranny of the majority. Together with other branches of governments, the domestic court system plays a specific, balanced role in the legitimisation of the exercise of public power. For this reason, judicial review is embedded in institutional structures that ensure the continuity and consistency of jurisprudence, as well as a due respect for the prerogatives of other branches of government. Arguably, investor-state arbitration does not form part of these constitutional arrangements.[101] Rather, it is an external mechanism provided with the mere purpose of soothing investor concerns over the quality of domestic adjudication. It is an extra-constitutional form of review of government conduct, provided exclusively for the benefit of foreign investors and without repercussions for the domestic legitimacy of governance. For this reason, international investment protection has been compared to a political risk insurance.[102] As noted by Benedikt Pirker, investment arbitration pursues 'the logic of an insurance policy for investors which offers the determination of a breach and calculation of compensation *ex post*'.[103] Consequently, the main task of tribunals is to provide appropriate compensation, rather than to re-assess 'the balancing of interests undertaking by a legislator or administrator in order to suggest a "better" balance'.[104]

The limited scope and function of arbitral review distinguishes investment arbitration from public law review, even though both types of proceedings involve the evaluation of government conduct. Whereas judicial review serves to control the legitimate exercise of public power by legislative and executive branches of government within a constitutional framework, investment arbitration entails a mechanism specifically aimed at settling disputes between a host state and an investor concerning the former's treaty commitments.[105] This difference affects the desirability of deference in

---

101. This seems to distinguish investment arbitration from standing international courts, such as the European Court of Human Rights, the World Trade Organization Dispute Settlement Bodies and the European Court of Justice, which have a more 'constitutional' role. See Alec Stone Sweet and Thomas L Brunell, 'Trustee Courts and the Judicialization of International Regimes. The Politics of Majoritarian Activism in the ECHR, the EU, and the WTO' (2013) *Yale Law School Faculty Scholarship Series*. Paper 4625 <http://digitalcommons.law.yale.edu/fss_papers/4625> accessed 1 July 2015.
102. Subedi 2008, *supra* note 73, 89. For certain differences, see Kaj Hobér and Joshua Fellenbaum, 'Political Risk Insurance and Investment Treaty Protection' in Bungenberg 2015, *supra* note 68, 1517-1551.
103. Pirker 2013, *supra* note 14, 347.
104. *Ibid*. See also Pieter Bekker and Akiko Ogawa, 'The Impact of Bilateral Investment Treaty (BIT) Proliferation on Demand for Investment Insurance: Reassessing Political Risk Insurance After the "BIT Bang"' (2013) 28 *ICSID Review* 2, 314-350. Bekker and Ogawa argue that the protection offered by BITs is substantially similar to that offered by political risk insurance, although they did not find a causal link between BIT proliferation and demand for political risk insurance.
105. Katselas 2012, *supra* note 12, 147: 'the function performed by investment tribunals should not be regarded as equal to the administrative review function, and certainly not to the constitutional-review

international investment law.[106] In the municipal context, deference ensures a legitimate allocation of public power among different branches of government. Investment arbitration, however, does not concern the constitutional legitimacy of government conduct, but only the host state's compliance with treaty standards. Consequently, the major justification for deference in the domestic context, the logic of the separation of powers, does not apply in international investment law. While arbitral tribunals may issue condemning awards that require the host state to pay compensation, this does not affect the domestic balance of powers between the different actors in the constitutional scheme.

3.6 CONCLUDING REMARKS

There are few fields of law in which the legitimacy of different forms of dispute resolution is as topical as it is in international investment law today. Within this field, the practice of investor-state arbitration has come under growing criticism for its alleged infringements on national sovereignty and its prioritisation of private over public interests. It has been argued that the legitimacy of the current regime could be reinforced if tribunals would adopt a deferential approach to the review of contested domestic measures. Similar approaches have been developed by domestic administrative and constitutional courts who exercise judicial review.

This chapter has found, however, that the function of investment arbitration is different from that of domestic judicial review. Whereas judicial review serves to ensure the legitimacy of government action within the constitutional framework, investment arbitration has a more narrow function. Its main purpose is to give investors the opportunity to obtain indemnification for losses caused by unforeseeable host state conduct. It is offered in order to sooth investor concerns about regulatory change and other state measures that would hamper the profitability of the investment. Certainly, arbitral review of government conduct involves a certain degree of evaluation, but unlike domestic judicial review, it does not influence the balance of power between different branches of government, which is where the logic of deference originates from.

---

function, performed by national courts. Investment arbitration is an alternative to a host state's courts that foreign investors may choose in the event of a dispute with the state, but it is no substitute for judicial review'. For Katselas, however, the differences between arbitral and judicial review provide a reason for even greater deference in the context of investment arbitration.

106. James Egerton-Vernon argues that deference actually comprises the legitimacy of investor-state arbitration. Egerton-Vernon 2010, *supra* note 43, 204: 'Tribunals must reject the application of inappropriate public law standards of review and instead revert to the strict application of the provisions of the international treaties governing their disputes. Only through thereby returning investment law to its private law roots can it perform the function for which it was created'. Egerton-Vernon argues that it should be left to states to reform the current system as they see fit.

The narrow approach to investor-state arbitration described so far may soothe some of the concerns raised against it in recent times. In response to the fear that investor-state arbitration threatens democratic decision-making, it could be emphasised that the evaluation of state policies undertaken by arbitral tribunals is of a different nature than the one undertaken by administrative and constitutional courts. Moreover, the alleged intrusion into sovereignty could be put into perspective by the fact that an arbitral award does not touch upon the legality of state measures in the domestic legal order, but only results in the indemnification of the investor.

The argument proposed here is different from the public law approach to international investment law. According to the latter perspective, the legitimacy of investor-state arbitration can be enhanced if arbitral tribunals would act more like domestic courts involved in the judicial review of state action. It is argued here, however, that the legitimacy of investor-state arbitration would be better served by a sharper distinction between the functions of arbitral tribunals on the one hand and domestic courts on the other hand. Conceiving investor-state arbitration as the international counterpart of administrative law review may actually threaten the legitimacy of the international investment law regime, because it turns arbitral tribunals into administrators of global governance and, consequently, expands their authority beyond the settlement of investor claims, which was their original mandate.

4 | PEOPLE'S MEDIATION IN CHINA: A SUPPLEMENT TO LITIGATION

*Liuhu Luo**

4.1 INTRODUCTION

Mediation (*tiaojie*) has a long history in China. As a non-judicial method of dispute resolution, people's mediation is termed as 'a flower of the East'.[1] China traditionally regards disputes as an impediment to social harmony while it considers mediation as an amicable way to tackle disputes without undermining social stability.[2] The approaches of solving civil disputes in China could be divided into two catalogues: judicial procedure and alternative dispute resolution. The former comprises adjudication and judicial mediation (*sifa tiaojie*)[3], whilst the latter covers arbitration, administrative mediation (*xingzheng tiaojie*)[4], and people's mediation (*renmin tiaojie*).[5]

---

* PhD Candidate, Maastricht University.
1. Rob Jagtenberg, Annie De Roo, 'The "New" Mediation: Flower of the East in a Harvard Bouquet' [2001] Asia Pacific Law Review 63.
2. It is generally acknowledged that Confucianism has a considerable influence on Chinese preference of solving disputes in a harmonious way. See James A. Wall, Michael Blum, 'Community Mediation in the People's Republic of China' [1991] Journal of Conflict Resolution 3, 4; Zeng Xianyi, 'Mediation in China – Past and Present' [2009] Asia Pacific Law Review 1, 2. Besides, a brief history of the people's mediation could be found in: Gabrielle Kaufmann-Kohler, Fan Kun, 'Integrating Mediation into Arbitration: Why it Works in China' [2008] Journal of International Arbitration 479, 483-484.
3. In China legal practice, judicial mediation is a process presided over by judges during the judicial trial, and the mediation is based on the parties' voluntary consent. As a result, the People's Court will make a mediation agreement rather than a judgment in solving the disputes, most of which are civil disputes. To have more details of judicial mediation, please see, Wang Liming, 'Characteristics of China's Judicial Mediation System' [2009] Asia Pacific Law Review 67. The 'litigation mediation' or 'court's mediation' is another terminology which is synonymous with the term 'judicial mediation'. Please see, Zhi Wu, 'Litigation Mediation for Intellectual Property Disputes in Chinese Local Courts: Experiences and Contradictions' [2009] Asia Pacific Law Review 117.
4. Administrative mediation mainly refers to a process chaired by relevant administrative organs in resolving civil disputes (such as marriage or contract disputes) and certain criminal cases. To have an overview of administrative mediation, please see, Yu Jianlong, 'Conciliation in Action in China and CIETAC's Practice' [2009] Asia Pacific Law Review 89, 89-91.
5. There are other similar terminology utilized to describe '*renmin tiaojie*', such as 'community mediation'. In this contribution, I use the term 'people's mediation'.

People's mediation is a process that a people's mediation committee (*renmin tiaojie weiyuanhui*) advises parties to resolve disputes through reaching a mediation agreement based on equal negotiation and free will. As an informal and extrajudicial approach, people's mediation solves disputes with the assistance of third parties, respects disputants' desire to select mediators, and imposes no costs.[6] During mediation, mediators often try to facilitate a compromise between disputants by advising or counseling.[7] Unlike a judgment, a mediation agreement does not have binding force upon parties. A mediation agreement mainly depends on the parties' voluntary enforcement. Since 1954, China has gradually launched the system of people's mediation, the framework of which has been reshaped by People's Mediation Act of the People's Republic of China (hereinafter, People's Mediation Act).

People's mediation has long been deemed as an important method for settling civil disputes in Chinese legal practice.[8] It mainly entertains civil cases like contract disputes, marital disputes, consumer protection, and torts. Notably people's mediation is also utilized to mediate minor criminal cases or administrative disputes between governments and individuals.[9] In recent years, people's mediation has been incorporated into the so-called Big Mediation (*da tiaojie*) network. The Supreme People's Court aimed to establish a channel of communication and assistance between people's mediation and litigation. The scope of people's mediation is extended to prior court trial under the Big Mediation network.[10] Some suggest that such changes display the trend of China's 'turning against law'.[11] In October 2014, the Communist

---

6. To know more about the merits of mediation, please see, Elsie Leung, 'Mediation-A Cultural Change' [2009] Asia Pacific Law Review 39, 43-44.
7. Please see Article 2 of People's Mediation Act 2010.
8. Supreme People's Court, Notice of the Supreme People's Court on Issuing Several Opinions on Further Implementing the Work Principle of 'Giving Priority to Mediation and Combining Mediation with Judgment' (*Guanyu Jinyibu Guanche Tiaojie Youxian Tiaopan Jiehe Gongzuo Yuanze De Ruogan Yijian*), No. 16 in 2010.
9. Under the slogan 'where are disputes, there is people's mediation', people's mediation is likely to enjoy a rather wide material scope. During the deliberation on the proposal of People's Mediation Act, some members of the congress proposed to set forth a definition of the scope of application. Nevertheless, the legislators did not deem it necessary to do so, and instead they empowered mediation committees with discretionary power. The consideration is that the types and contents of disputes are distinct in different districts, and new disputes keep emerging with the social and economic development. Consequently, People's Mediation Act adopted the terminology of 'disputes among the people', so as to extend the scope of people's mediation. See Aaron Halegua, 'Reforming the People's Mediation System in Urban China' [2005] Hong Kong Law Journal 2005, p.739.
10. In Chinese, it is called '大调解' (*da tiaojie*). In this contribution, I refer to it as 'big mediation'. Nonetheless, some scholars translate it as 'grand mediation' or 'multipartite mediation'. See Zhao Jingbo, 'People's Mediation System Perfection and Reform under the Multipartite Mediation Mechanism' [2012] Cross-Cultural Communication 87, 87-91. Jieren Hu, 'Grand mediation in China' [2011] Asian Survey 1065, 1065–1089. Jieren Hu, Lingjian Zeng, 'Grand mediation and legitimacy enhancement in contemporary China – the Guang'an model' [2014] Journal of Contemporary China.
11. Carl F Minzner, 'China's Turn against Law' [2011] American Journal of Comparative Law 935, 935-984.

Party of China (CPC) convened the Fourth Plenary Session of 18th CPC Central Committee. It was the first time in CPC history to focus on the theme of rule of law in China at plenary meeting.[12] What will be the possible implications generated by the decision of 'comprehensively advancing the rule of law'?[13] Against this background, it is the right time to critically review the changes of people's mediation and the relationship between people's mediation and adjudication.

Accordingly, the paper first gives an overview of the recent developments of people's mediation, discussing the increased role of private actors in people's mediation system (Section 4.2). Subsequently, it explores the legitimacy of the foregoing changes and reform of people's mediation from the perspectives of culture, politics, and sociology (Section 4.3). The paper continues to formulate the relationship between people's mediation and litigation (Section 4.4). Sections 4.5 and 4.6 analyze the defects of people's mediation, make comments on its future development, and deliver a conclusion.

4.2 THE INCREASED POSITION OF PRIVATE ACTORS IN PEOPLE'S MEDIATION

4.2.1 Introduction

Before proceeding, it is helpful to have an overview of people's mediation committees first. Article 7 of People's Mediation Act reads that: 'people's mediation commissions are mass-based organizations legally formed to settle disputes among the people.' In this regard, a people's mediation committee is neither an administrative organ nor a judicial organ in nature. Villagers' committees[14] and urban residents committees[15] must establish people's mediation committees, while enterprises and public institu-

---

12. Wang Cong, 'Xinhua Insight: CPC Convenes First Plenum on "Rule of Law" in Reform, Anti-Graft Drive' (*Sina English*, 20 October 2014) <http://news.xinhuanet.com/english/indepth/2014-10/20/c_133729667.htm> accessed 15 June 2015.
13. An English transaltion of the documents adopted by the Plenary Session could be found in the following website. Compilation and Translation Bureau of the Central Committee of the Communist Party of China, 'Communique of the Fourth Plenary Session of the 18th Central Committee of the Communist Party of China' (*China.org.cn*, 2 December 2014) <www.china.org.cn/china/fourth_plenary_session/2014-12/02/content_34208801.htm> accessed 9 August 2015.
14. In the light of Article 2 of Organic Law of the Villagers' Committees of the People's Republic of China (2010 Revision), a villagers committee is a primary mass organization of self-government. Its sub-paragraph reads that: "The villagers committee shall manage the public affairs and public welfare undertakings of the village, mediate disputes among the villagers, help maintain public order, and convey the villagers' opinions and demands and make suggestions to the people's government."
15. According to Article 2 of Organic Law of the Urban Residents Committee of the People's Republic of China (1989), an urban residents committee is a mass organization for self-government at the grassroots level. An urban residents committee has the responsibility of (i) handling the public affairs and public

tions[16] have the discretion to decide whether to launch such committees or not.[17] In 2009, there were 42,000 people's mediation committees around China, and 12,000 industrial and other kinds of mediation committees were established by social groups.[18] By 2013, the numbers of committees and people's mediators respectively rose to 817,000 and 4.28 million.[19]

With regard to the forms of people's mediation committee, there are three major changes. Firstly, people's mediation committees have not only been established in villagers, neighborhoods, enterprises, and public institutions, but they have also been constructed in people's courts and police stations, the places that are confronted with an explosion of disputes. Secondly, specialized or industrial mediation committees have been introduced to resolve disputes between hospitals and patients, securities firms and shareholders, and so on.[20] Thirdly, people's mediation has become an important part of the Big Mediation network. Accordingly, the position of private actors in people's mediation regime is being raised. The following section describes these private actors in people's mediation.

4.2.2   *Private Actors in People's Mediation*

People's mediation involves many players, mainly including people's mediation committees, people's mediators, disputants, local governments, and local courts.[21] As a non-governmental organization, a people's mediation committee is often composed of (i) members of people's committees; (ii) mediators; and (iii) relatives, neighbors, or colleagues of the parties concerned, who are invited by a mediator upon the parties' consent.[22] Besides, retired judges, academics, and lawyers gradually play an active role in people's mediation. Recent years have witnessed the rise of new-fashioned and

welfare services of the residents in the local residential area; (ii) mediating disputes among the residents; and (iii) assisting in the maintenance of public security.

16. In accordance with Article 2 of Interim Regulation on the Registration of Public Institutions (2004 Revision), public institutions 'refers to the public service organizations that are established by the state organs or other organizations by using the state-owned assets for the purpose of engaging in activities of education, science and technology, culture and hygiene'.

17. See Article 8 of People's Mediation Act.

18. Wang Shengmin and Hao Chiyong (eds), *Interpretation of People's Mediation Act of People's Republic of China, Law Press China (Zhonghua Renmin Gongheguo Renmin Tiaojiefa Shiyi)* (Law Press 2010) 65-68.

19. Liangjie, 'There Are 0,817 Million People's Mediation Organizations Nationwide and the Success Rate of Mediation in 2012 Is 96% (*Quanguo Gongyou Renmin Tiaojie Zuzhi 0,817 Baiwan Ge)'* (*Guangming Net*, 28 August 2013) <http://politics.gmw.cn/2013-08/28/content_8730678.htm> accessed 15 June 2015.

20. Liu Min, 'On Innovation and Development of People's Mediation System (Renmin Tiaojie Zhidu De Chuangxin Yu Fazhan)' [2012] Law Science Magazine 60.

21. John S Mo, 'Understanding the Role of People's Mediation in the Age of Globalization' [2009] Asia Pacific Law Review 75, 78.

22. See Articles 8, 13, and 20 of People's Mediation Act.

professional mediation organizations. For example, as a self-regulation organization, the Securities Association of China established the Mediation Center of Securities Disputes. The center is mainly responsible for mediating disputes relating to stock exchange transactions.[23] In this sense, private actors in this context not only refer to individuals, but also point at nongovernmental groups or organizations.

4.2.2.1   Mediators

Mediators of people's mediation usually come from members of people's mediation committees. A people's mediation committee comprises three to nine members. There will be one director, but the committee will appoint two or more deputy directors if the appointment is of necessity. As for villagers' committees and residents committees, the members of corresponding mediation committee shall respectively be elected through villagers' meetings, villagers' representative meetings, or residents' meetings. As to the mediation committees in enterprises and public institutions, members shall be elected by employee's assemblies, employee's representative meetings, or labor unions. Besides, the term of office of members is 3 years, and the members could be reelected when the term is expired.[24] What's more, Article 8 of People's Mediation Act stipulates that: 'A people's mediation committee shall have female members and, as in an area of multiethnic population, have members from ethnic minorities.'

Article 19 of the People's Mediation Act provides two ways for the selection of mediators. Before mediation, a people's mediation committee may designate one or more mediators, or the parties concerned may select one or more mediators themselves. There are three requirements for becoming a people's mediator (*renmin tiaojieyuan*): (i) he or she shall be an adult citizen, namely at least 18 years old according to Chinese civil law; (ii) he or she shall be impartial, decent, and dedicated to mediation; and (iii) he or she shall have knowledge of state policy and law. In practice, mediators and disputers may come from the same village, neighborhood, or working place, and may know each other well or have a close relationship. It is said that 'most mediators are local villagers or local residents who have great knowledge about their own villages, local residents, village rules and folk regulations, and customs'.[25]

4.2.2.2   Other Individuals

People's mediators are entitled to invite individuals to participate in mediation process. Only after getting the consent of the parties can people's mediators invite private organizations or individuals. Specifically speaking, there are three kinds of persons that could be invited. The first is relatives, neighbors, or colleagues of the parties

---

23. See Articles 8 and 12 of the Administrative Measures on Securities Dispute Mediation (for Trial Implementation) (*Zhongguo Zhengquanye Xiehui Zhengquan Jiufen Tiaojie Gongzuo Guanli Banfa (Shixing)*), 11 June 2012.
24. See Articles 8 and 9 of People's Mediation Act.
25. Zhao (n 2) 89.

concerned; the second is persons with specialized knowledge or experiences, such as a retired judge or a law professor; the third is persons coming from relevant social organizations. Furthermore, people's mediation committees encourage local citizens who are fair and honest, keen on mediation, and popular with the masses, to initiatively apply to participate in the mediation process.[26] These people may enjoy a rather high prestige in local community, which will contribute to a quicker resolution of disputes. Consequently, people's mediation committees welcome their participation through providing convenience and working conditions for them. In addition, these people could also be foreigners who work or live in China, especially where a dispute involves foreigners. Wang and Hao argue that foreigners, who have certain knowledge about foreign legislation, customs, or Chinese law, can obtain foreigners' confidence easier.[27] Nevertheless, the invitation shall be also agreed by the parties.

4.2.2.3   Specialized Mediation Organizations

People's mediation is moving towards professionalism – mediators and organizations with expert knowledge are much needed and welcomed.[28] Traditionally, people's mediation is targeted at quarrels and conflicts between villagers or residents. With social changes of China, disputes emerge more often between strangers from different districts, and the types of disputes are increasingly complicated. Thus, neighborhood committees and villagers' committees play a less important role in people's mediation, while professional mediation committees are increasingly needed.[29] For example, with the increase of medical disputes, mediation committees comprising medical experts spring up. In order to facilitate the specialization of mediation, the Ministry of Justice released two Opinions in 2011 and 2014, respectively.[30] From 2011 to 2014,

---

26. Fei Xiaotong described in 1948 the occasion of mediation in rural China as follows. "I have been asked to attend meetings where I was to help mediate quarrels. In the villagers' view, it was very natural that I should be invited to do so. I am a teacher. Therefore, I read books. Therefore, I must understand rituals. Therefore, I must be an authority in this respect. The other mediators were the village elders. One of the most interesting things about these meetings was that the baozhang, the government's representative in the village, never spoke. And the reason he did not speak was that he had no social status in the village at all. He was just a petty bureaucrat. What we now call 'mediation' (*tiaojie*) used to be called 'critical reasoning' (*pingli*)."
Fei Xiaotong continued to describe that the procedure will be chaired by "the same extremely articulate local notable". The chair will start the procedure by scolding both disputants. And he would lecture them about what was wrong and what should be done for the possible reconciliation. See Fei Xiaotong, *From the Soil: The Foundations of Chinese Society* (Gary G. Hamilton and Wang Zheng University of California Press 1992) 103-104.
27. Wang, Hao (n 18) 67-68.
28. Jagtenberg, De Roo (n 1) 74-79.
29. Zhu Jingwen, 'Data Analysis of Flow of Litigation into Different Channels in China' [2009] Social Sciences in China 100, 117.
30. Ministry of Justice, Opinions of the Ministry of Justice on Strengthening the Building of Industry-based and Profession-based People's Mediation Committees (*Sifabu Guanyu Jiaqiang Hangyexing Zhuanyexing Renmin Tiaojie Weiyuanhui Jianshe De Yijian*), No. 93 in 2011.

more than 30,000 mediation organizations of guilds or professional mediation organizations[31] were established around China, with almost 130,000 mediators. During this period, there are more than 3 million cases solved through these industry-based or profession-based mediation organizations.[32] This phenomenon could be illustrated as follows.

On the one hand, the Ministry of Justice seeks to introduce people's mediation into more fields through launching special mediation organizations.[33] Social organizations and other groups could establish specialized or industrial mediation committees in cities, counties, towns or neighborhoods, or initiate mediation workroom in companies and other units.[34] Against this background, self-regulation organizations start to launch mediation committees within the guilds. For example, the Securities Association of China established the Mediation Center of Securities Disputes. The Ministry of Justice, the Ministry of Health and China Insurance Regulatory Commission cooperate to support the establishment of professional mediation committees targeted to disputes of medical treatments.[35] Additionally, some local governments buy nongovernmental mediation service by service contracts, making people's mediation become a kind of public service for local citizens. A telling example is the evolution of People's Mediation Studio of Li Qin established in 2003 in Shanghai. At the beginning, the studio was just a nongovernmental organization; now it is an enterprise with Li Qin, a retired woman, as the legal representative. The business area of the studio is mediation service of civil disputes. The studio concludes service contracts with local sub-district offices, providing service of people's mediation for residents.[36]

31. By December 2013, there were 2,418 people's mediation committees and 1,029 people's mediation studios, which are specially targeted at mediating medical treatment disputes. There are 22,802 mediators. From 2010 to September 2013, 228,000 cases were successfully mediated. See Ministry of Justice P.R.C, '2,418 People's Mediation Committees Were Established Nationwide in the Field of Medical Disputes, Covering Most of the Municipal Administrative Areas (*Quanguo Yi She Yiliao Jiufen Renmin Tiaojie Weiyuanhui 2,418 Ge, Jiben Fugai Dishi Yishang Xingzheng Quyu)*' (*Ministry of Justice P.R.C*, 26 December 2013) <www.moj.gov.cn/index/content/2013-12/26/content_5157510.htm?node=7343> accessed 15 June 2015.

32. Ministry of Justice, Opinions of the Ministry of Justice on Further Strengthening the Industry-based and Profession-based People's Mediation Works (*Sifabu Guanyu Jinyibu Jiaqiang Hangyexing Zhuanyexing Renmin Tiaojie Gongzuo De Yijian*), No. 109 in 2014.

33. Ibid.

34. Ministry of Justice (n 30).

35. See Opinions of the Ministry of Justice, the Ministry of Health, and China Insurance Regulatory Commission on Solving Medical Treatments Disputes through People's Mediation (*Sifabu Weishengbu Baojianhui Guanyu Jiaqiang Yiliao Jiufen Renmin Tiaojie Gongzuo De Yijian*), 8 January 2010.

36. Zhang Yongjin, 'Study on Mediation Studio in China – Comparison of the Patterns between Shanghai and Guang'an (*Zhongguo Tiaojie Gongzuoshi Zhidu Yanjiu – Jiyu Shanghai Yu Guang'an Moshi De Kaocha*) [2011] Journal of Sichuan University of Science & Engineering (Social Sciences Edition) 54, 55-56.

On the other hand, the Ministry of Justice stresses the necessity of considering specific industrial features and circumstances when launching mediation organizations. It is proposed to appoint full-time mediators and build expert databases comprising academics or specialists. It is stressed that mediators of these organizations shall be selected from people who are experts in the field at issue and are also experienced in law or psychology.[37] For instance, the Management Measure of Mediators in Electricity Power Disputes stipulates that mediators shall not only be familiar with legislation and policy on electricity power, but also should have professional knowledge on electricity power and economics.[38] What's more, such mediation committees are encouraged to launch platforms, enabling retired judges, prosecutors, lawyers, notaries, professors, or experts to contribute to mediation.[39]

4.2.3   The Network of Big Mediation

The Supreme People's Court proposed to construct a linkage of mediation framework constituted by both state organs and private actors. The Big Mediation network was thus encouraged and promoted. The Big Mediation network unites together judicial mediation, administrative mediation, and people's mediation in the process of resolution of disputes.[40] The word 'big' highlights the widespread nature of the network and the large amount of players getting involved in mediation process.

There are four remarkable features of the Big Mediation system. Firstly, the network is led by the Communist Party of China. Secondly, many different actors (including but not limited to courts, governments, and people's mediation committees) work jointly to solve specific disputes. Thirdly, it not only offers *ex post facto* remedies for parties as the court does, but also provides ex-ante precaution measures against the emergence of all kinds of disputes.[41] Fourthly, courts provide a platform for mediation. Courts are entitled to invite or entrust those organizations, which are entitled to mediate civil disputes, to participate in the mediation before or even after people's courts' registering the cases. During the process of solving disputes, it requires local courts to cooperate with organizations such as villagers' committees, residents committees, labor unions, communist youth leagues, women federations, etc.

In particular, as for the cases falling into people's courts' jurisdiction, courts may invite administrative organs, people's mediation organizations, and commercial

---

37. Ministry of Justice (n 30).
38. State Electricity Regulatory Commission, Management Measures of Mediators in Electronic Power Disputes (*Dianli Zhengyi Tiaojieyuan Guanli Banfa*) 2005.
39. Ministry of Justice (n 30).
40. Supreme People's Court (n 8).
41. Ai Jiahui, 'The Function and Application Scope of 'Grand Mediation' (*Datioajie De Yunzuo Moshi Yu Shiyong Bianjie*)' [2011] Studies in Law and Business 19.

mediation organizations to advise disputants to settle conflicts through mediation. This invitation could be sent out on the courts' own decision or the
parties' request. If disputants reject mediation or if they cannot reach a mediation agreement within a fixed time, the court shall hear the case. Based on the
parties' consent or the court's decision, the court may entrust administrative
organs, people's mediation organizations, commercial mediation organizations
to assist the court in mediation. Besides, the parties concerned are allowed to
select which organs or organizations to join mediation, or they could request
the court's appointment of such participants. If the parties reach an agreement
during mediation, they could withdraw the lawsuit or request the court to con-
firm the effectiveness of the agreement; otherwise, the court shall try the case
under judicial procedures.[42]

The Supreme People's Court has advocated constructing a database of specially
invited mediators and mediation volunteers, which is mainly composed of deputies
to the people's congress, members of the people's political consultative committees,
judicial assessors, and retired government leaders.[43] Additionally, the Supreme People's Court launched a pilot project in 42 local courts.[44] Firstly, people's mediation
organizations may build a mediation workroom in people's courts. Such a workroom
mainly comprises people's mediators, but it will also invite judges to join the mediation when there is necessity. The main function of the workroom is to carry out mediation upon the courts' invitation, and to provide another choice of solving disputes for
parties, thus alleviating the caseload of courts. Because such mediation usually happens before the disputes have been heard by the court, it is called pretrial mediation.[45]
Secondly, these courts shall launch a register system for the specially invited mediation organizations, and formulate the requirements for administrative organs, people's mediation organizations, and commercial mediation organizations to become
specially invited mediation organizations. Thirdly, these courts shall construct a register system for these specially invited mediators, and formulate the requirements for
private individuals (including but not limited to deputies to congress, judicial

---

42. See Articles 14 and 15 of the Notice of the Supreme People's Court on Issuing the Overall Plan on Expan-
    ding the Pilot Reform of Dispute Resolution Mechanisms by Coordination between Litigation and Non-
    Litigation (Guanyu Kuoda Susong Yu Fei Susong Xiang Xianjie De Maodun Jiufen Jiejue Jizhi Gaige
    Shidian Zongti Fangan) 2012.
43. Supreme People's Court (n 8).
44. The following three points of the pilot project are based on the document of the Supreme People's Court
    (n 40).
45. See the Notice of the Supreme People's Court on Issuing Several Opinions on Further Implementing the
    Work Principle of 'Giving Priority to Mediation and Combining Mediation with Judgment' (Guanyu
    Jinyibu Guanche Tiaojie Youxian Tiaopan Jiehe Gongzuo Yuanze De Ruogan Yijian), No. 16 in 2010; Guiding
    Opinions of the Supreme People's Court on Comprehensively Promoting the Construction of Litigation
    Service Centers in the People's Courts (Zuigao Renmin Fayuan Guanyu Quanmian Tuijin Renmin
    Fayuan Susong Fuwu Zhongxin Jianshe De Zhidao Yijian), 15 December 2014.

assessors, academics, and lawyers) to become a specially invited mediator. Lawyers associations and law firms are encouraged to initiate platforms for lawyers to act as mediators chairing mediation process.

4.2.4   Summary

To summarize, people's mediation has become a significant channel of dispute resolution, with an increased role of private actors played in mediation. People's mediation moves towards specialized or industrial mediation. The selection of Mediators are no longer limited to members of mediation committees; instead, different individuals are invited to join the mediation procedure. Another important change is the construction of the Big Mediation network, getting public actors and private actors involved in mediation process. It is believed that the establishment of the Big Mediation system will smooth the cooperation between people's mediation and adjudication, minimizing the drawbacks of 'single-method dispute resolution' and better tackling disputes.[46] Nevertheless, the practical implications generated by such changes are still not sure. How does this system uphold both public interests and private interests? This is a question that still to be answered. There are doubts that governmental departments in the Big Mediation are like a double-edged sword – either protecting the interest of individuals or suppressing disputes which harm the interest of governments.[47] In the light of this concern, the following section analyzes the legitimacy of these changes.

4.3   THE LEGITIMACY OF PEOPLE'S MEDIATION

This section proceeds to explore the legitimacy of the emphasis on people's mediation and the increased position of private actors. It argues that there are cultural, political, and social impetuses for the evolution of people's mediation. From the perspective of culture, Confucius' philosophy of harmony lays the foundation for people's mediation and gradually has an impact on Chinese people's preference of choice of solving disputes.[48] Politics have an aspiration to maintain social harmony, thus people's mediation is considered as a supplementary to litigation. Dramatic social changes in China lead to distrust of litigation, which urge China to establish a diversified regime of dispute resolution. Last but not least, party autonomy is a specific characteristic of people's mediation, making the regime attractive.

---

46. Hu (n 10) 1070-1076.
47. Ibid.
48. Jun Ge, 'Mediation, Arbitration and Litigation: Dispute Resolution in the People's Republic of China' [1996] Pacific Basin Law Journal 122,123.

4.3.1   Social Harmony – Cultural and Political Root of People's Mediation

There is a connection between culturally shared values and the approach of dispute resolution.[49] It is worth researching what is the underlying cultural driving force for people's mediation. It is commonly believed that its cultural root is the Confucianism, which has made an indelible mark on the behavior of Chinese people.[50] There are two aspects that deserve attention. On the one hand, as one of the greatest philosophers in ancient China, Confucius (551-479 B.C.) considered the harmony (*he*) as the ideal social state. The harmony in this context means a friendly relationship between man and nature, man and Heaven, and man and man.[51] The pursuit of harmony encourages individuals to settle disputes through reaching compromise. Confucius illustrated his dream of building a society 'without litigation' by saying that: 'At hearing lawsuits I am like anybody else. What is necessary is to cause the people to have no lawsuits.'[52] On the other hand, Confucius placed great weight on 'virtue' in ruling the country and solving conflicts.[53] Informal dispute resolution methods (e.g., private mediation) rather than litigation are more preferred by people living in rural areas.[54] In turn, such reluctance interferes with the position of litigation in both social life and traditional politics. Ordinary people tend to choose other methods to solve disputes. Particularly, some may regard going to court as an embarrassing experience. As a Chinese proverb says, family troubles are not a thing to be talked about in public (*Jiachou Buke Waiyang*). In this context, mediation offers another choice.

Politics in modern China stick to the ideal of preserving social harmony. But they gradually place the establishment of a country ruled by law on agenda. The Communist Party of China (CPC) announced to launch the 'harmonious society' (*hexie shehui*) in 2005, with an aim of addressing social disparities and conflicts facing modern

---

49. "The varieties of dispute settlement, and the socially sanctioned choices in any culture, communicate the ideals people cherish, their perceptions of themselves, and the quality of their relationships with others. See Jerold S. Auerbach, *Justice without Law?* (Oxford University Press 1983) 3-4.
50. Wall, Blum (n 2) 4-11. Jun Ge (n 48).
51. For instance, Confucius said, "In practicing the rules of propriety, it is harmony that it is prized." Confucius said "The superior man has no competition." See Yang Bojun etc., *The Analects of Confucius* (Chinese-English bilingual edition, Qi Lu Press 1993) 7-21.
52. Ibid 137.
53. The Master said that: "If the people are guided by virtue, and kept in order by the rules of propriety, they will have a sense of shame, and moreover will come to be good." And the Master stated that "The man of perfect virtue is one who, desiring to sustain himself, sustains others, and desiring to develop himself, develops others. To be able to draw from one's self a parallel for the treatment of others, that may be called the way to practice virtue." In addition, the 'rule of virtue' is founded on the rituals (li). "Rituals are publicly recognized behavioral norms. If one behaves according to the rituals, then one's behavior is correct and proper." The rituals are maintained by people's 'feeling of respect and of obedience', while laws are enforced through state power. See Ibid 11-65. Fei (n 26) 96-98.
54. Vicki Waye, Ping Xiong, 'The Relationship between Mediation and Judicial Proceedings in China' [2011] Asian Journal of Comparative Law 1, 2-8.

China.[55] The harmonious society is expected to be a society that is "democratic and ruled by law, fair and just, trustworthy and fraternal, full of vitality, stable and orderly, and maintains harmony between man and nature."[56] Political expectation has a profound influence on the legitimacy of people's mediation. It is argued that mediation or people's mediation is not only a means to solve disputes, but also a way of "imposing Communist Party ideology".[57] Recent reforms (e.g., the introduction of Big Mediation) of people's mediation could be explained by political aspiration for keeping social harmony.

It should be noted that the promotion of people's mediation does not deny the importance of litigation. As a formal procedure based on state power, litigation is surely the last resort of solving disputes. The main challenge is how to make sure mediation becomes a supplement rather than an alternative to litigation. Both litigation and people's mediation become instruments for enhancing social harmony and stability.

4.3.2   *Social Changes – The Desire for Establishing Diversified Mechanisms of Dispute Resolution*

Since 1978, China has made tremendous economic and social achievements. Nonetheless, Chinese society has also experienced a transitional period, which is characterized by, *inter alia*, an increasing number of social disputes, environmental challenges, and distrust of judicial systems. People's courts at various levels are confronted with an increasing caseload.[58] With the explosion of caseload, the court is under great pressure.

Courts are being faced with social doubts of judicial justice, their adjudications are often criticized by litigants or academics. There are situations in which although the judges try the civil disputes or criminal cases strictly in accordance with law,

---

55. For instance, the Party pays attention to the issues of uneven economic development, social security, wealth distribution, and education etc. See Ai Guo Han, 'Building a Harmonious Society and Achieving Individual Harmony' [2008] Journal of Chinese Political Science, 143,144. Kin-man Chan, 'Harmonious Society', *International Encyclopedia of Civil Society* (2010) 821-825.
56. Ibid.
57. Waye, Xiong (n 54). Stanley Lubman, *Bird in A Cage: Legal Form in China after Mao* (Stanford University Press 2002) 59.
58. In the last 5 years (from 2008 to 2012), the Supreme People's Court entertained 50,773 cases, of which 49,863 cases were closed within the trial time limit. And the local people's courts at various levels accepted 56,105 million cases, and winded up 55,259 million cases, with a clearance rate of 98.8%. Besides, in the first 9 months of 2013, the people's courts registered 9,904,346 million cases, and the numbers of the lawsuits settled were 8,511,448 million, with an increasing rate of 3.85% and 2.91% respectively. Supreme People's Court, 'The Work Report of the Supreme People's Court on the First Session of the Twelfth National People's Congress (*Zuigao Renmin Fayuan Gongzuo Baogao, Di Shierjie Quanguo Renmin Daibiao Dahui Diyici Huiyi*)' (10 March 2013). For more and latest statistics, see the homepage of the Supreme People's Court <www.court.gov.cn/fabu.html>.

relevant judgments were finally overturned by higher people's courts or the Supreme People's Court. One of the reasons is the mass media's emotional responses, and this 'trial by media' phenomenon may mislead the public and undermine the authority of the judicial system.[59] Ironically, the role of law is a necessary but not a sufficient approach to cope with the disputes in China. The sole reliance on formal adjudication is far from enough.[60] The courts and their judgments fail to gain the trust from citizens, who have a deep doubt about social justice.

Another challenge is that China experiences a period when new types of civil cases spring up. Formerly, people's mediation mainly dealt with civil disputes. However, the common disputes in the transforming China are those that easily evoke the sentiment of the masses and affect social harmony.[61] Traditional people's mediation lacks the ability and experience to deal with such new types of disputes.[62] The frequent types of disputes have changed from traditional cases regarding marriage and family, neighborhood relationships, small claims of creditor's rights or slight torts to cases involving land expropriation, demolition and relocation of housing, environmental disputes, and medical claims.[63]

The problem is that such new types of conflicts cannot be effectively solved through an independent running of courts, local governments, or people's mediation committees. These kinds of conflicts involve masses of people and government departments, but China lacks a coordination mechanism in dispute resolution. This phenomenon impels the Chinese government to build a multi-layered dispute resolution mechanism, so as to realize the unification of social, legal and political effects through satisfactorily solving disputes.[64] As a result, the establishment of diversified mechanisms

---

59. One of the typical cases is People's Procuratorate of Guangzhou City v. Xuting on theft. Xuting is a man who worked for a company in Guangzhou City. One day when he withdrew money, he found that there may be something wrong with the ATM – when he chose to withdraw 1 yuan, he got 1,000 yuan from the ATM. He used the ATM for 171 times and finally took away 175,000 from the broken ATM. He then was on trial for theft and was sentenced to life in prison by the Court of First Instance of Guangzhou City. The judgment incurred many criticisms from academics and the media, arguing the sentence was unexpectedly harsh. The Court of Second Instance of Guangzhou City ordered the Court of First Instance to retry the case, and Xuting was sentenced to 5 years in prison in the retrial. See Gu Peidong, 'Legal analysis of Public Opinions on Trial: The Perspective of Xuting Case (Gongzhong Panyi De Fali Jieshi: Dui Xuting An De Yanshen Sikao)' [2008] China Legal Science, 167-178.
60. Julie Macfarlane etc. (eds), *Dispute Resolution: Readings and Case Studies* (Emond Montgomery Publication 2003)104.
61. Zhang Wusheng, 'The Establishment of China Grand Mediation System and its connection with ADR (Lun Woguo Datiaojie Jizhi De Goujian – Jian Xi Datiaojie Yu ADR De Guanxi)' [2007] Studies in Law and Business 111.
62. Hu (n 10) 1075.
63. Wang, Hao (n 18) 65.
64. Su Li, 'The "Judicial Activism" and extensive mediation (Guanyu Nengdong Sifa Yu Datiaojie)' [2010] China Legal Science 5.

of dispute resolution becomes a strong desire for China.[65] In October 2014, the CPC declared to construct a diversified, connective, and coordinating framework of conflicts resolution, which is made up of, *inter alia*, mediation, arbitration, administrative verdict, administrative review, and litigation. The CPC proposes to enhance the institutional development of industry-based or profession-based mediation organizations and to facilitate the linkage among people's mediation, administrative mediation, and judicial mediation.

In sum, in response to the social changes, there is a desire to introduce a new mediation system in accordance with the features of these areas or industries. It is in this context that the network of Big Mediation was created.

4.3.3   Party Autonomy – The Initiate of the Mediation Procedure

During mediation, people's mediation committees shall respect the parties' free will and the equality between the parties. Article 17 of People's Mediation Act enables disputants to apply for mediation themselves, and also allows people's committees to voluntarily propose mediation for disputers. However, no mediation shall be carried out if one party has expressly refused to settle a dispute through people's mediation. Apart from people's mediation, the parties are entitled to refer to arbitration, administrative means or judicial means for remedies. Mediators shall be neutral and not compel the parties to solve the disputes through mediation or reaching an agreement, otherwise such an agreement will be invalid.[66] Individual will is an important factor for the popularity of people's mediation. The advantages of people's mediation become a facilitating aspect for individuals, which could be explained as follows.

Firstly, mediators and disputants can enjoy more flexibility in procedures. For instance, a mediation committee could invite individuals, who are familiar with the disputers, to join the mediation based on practical needs. There is no doubt that the basis for their participation is the invitation and consent from the mediators and disputers respectively. The introduction of different people's mediation organizations, groups or individuals would facilitate the dialogue between disputers, which may help resolve the controversies while at the same time keep the parties' relationship as good as before.

Secondly, people's mediation provides regional and industrial convenience for the disputers. If the parties come from the same residents' community, they may choose the people's mediation organizations located in that neighborhood. Mediators often

---

65. Hu (n 10)1070.
66. Supreme People's Court, Some Provisions of the Supreme People's Court on Trying Civil Cases Involving the People's Conciliation Agreements (*Guanyu Shenli Sheji Renmin Tiaojie Xieyi De Minshi Anjian De Ruogan Guiding*), No. 29 in 2002.

live or work in the same neighborhoods, villages or enterprise, and have a close relationship with each other. In this regard, it saves both time and money for disputers to start a mediation process than to lodge a lawsuit.

Thirdly, people's mediation enables mediators to adopt distinct mediation methods according to the parties' personalities and the types of controversies.[67] Xiao Yang, the former president of the Supreme People's Court stressed that mediation would not just pay attention to legislation and logic, but take the sentiment (e.g., the parties' poor living conditions or financial situations) into consideration, thus making a balance between different parties' interests, and contributing to the social harmony.[68] In practice, a mediator may tell disputants to "consider the feelings of others, to cherish harmony in their families or community, and not to undermine the respect of the neighbors or the reputation of the family."[69] For example, as for marriage disputes, it may be more appropriate to have female mediators chair the mediation process, who were married and good at handling family affairs; in terms of disputes involving minorities, it may be more reasonable to have minority mediators to carry out mediation, which could help alleviate the minorities' concern of the mediators' justice.

Fourthly, people's mediation helps disputers preserve their reputation network through reaching mediation agreements. People do not want to disturb the harmonious relationship with kin and neighbors.[70] One significant distinction between adjudication and mediation is that the former is done 'by law', while the latter is done 'by human compassion'.[71] Generally speaking, adjudication draws a clear and inflexible line between right and wrong, while mediation leaves a space for a flexible compromise on disputes and remedies. It is believed that mediation can make a balance between law and feelings of disputants; and it is in this sense that mediation is considered as an appropriate way to resolve disputes without interfering with the harmonious relationship between neighbors, relatives, and friends, etc. In other words, people's mediation can help minimize hostility. As the saying goes, it is wiser to "keep a friend than win a victory".[72] On the other hand, during mediation,

---

67. Notice of the Supreme People's Court on Enhancing the Work of Retrial and Mediation (*Zuigao Renmin Fayuan Guanyu Jiaqiang Zaishen Tiaojie Gongzuo De Tongzhi*), No. 63 in 2005.
68. Ibid.
69. Wall, Blum (n 2) 4-11.
70. "The basic unit of traditional Chinese society was not the individual but the basic group to which those individuals belonged…. These social groups (the family, clan, village and guild) dominated the individual, and they generally strove to avoid involving government officials in quarrels between their members." See Kaufmann-Kohler, Kun (n 2) 481.
71. Philip C. C. Huang, *Civil Justice in China: Representation and Practice in the Qing* (Stanford University Press 1996) 204.
72. Ge (n 48) 123.

community values can be spread and individuals can learn from the mediated case, thus maintaining social harmony.[73]

4.4   PEOPLE'S MEDIATION IS A SUPPLEMENTARY TO LITIGATION

What is the relationship between people's mediation and adjudication? The starting point of the discussion is that people's mediation and adjudication have many differences in resolving disputes, but they together constitute a part of the dispute resolution regimes in China. They have different scopes of application. People's mediation mainly deals with civil disputes, administrative conflicts, and minor offences. But adjudication can address civil, administrative, and criminal cases. Furthermore, people's mediation is more flexible in procedure than what a trial can adopt. Besides, social morality, village regulations, customs, and industry practices could also be utilized in mediation to settle conflicts.[74] As regards litigation, national law is the primary source of law. However, such differences do not deny the connection and interaction between people's mediation and adjudication.

4.4.1   Two Coexisting Systems

The people's mediation and litigation are two coexisting system of disputes resolution. They each represent a way of solving disputes. Generally speaking, parties can choose to accept mediation or bring disputes before a court. According to the Law Yearbook of China,[75] during the period from 1981 to 2011, there were around 193 million cases handled through people's mediation while 126 million cases were tried by courts.[76] Without people's mediation, courts around China have to hear more cases. In this sense, people's mediation is considered as a method to alleviate the caseload of courts in China.[77]

4.4.2   Filling the Gaps Left by Litigation

People's mediation can step in the blank areas that are not regulated by law. For instance, civil law usually does not provide rules for how lovers shall cherish their

---

73. Jerome Alan Cohen, 'Chinese Mediation on the Eve of Modernization' [1966] California Law Review 1201, 1224. Fei (n 26) 104.

74. The Supreme People's Court, Notice of the Supreme People's Court on Issuing the Overall Plan on Expanding the Pilot Reform of Dispute Resolution Mechanisms by Coordination between Litigation and Non-Litigation, 2012.

75. The Law Yearbook of China is a series of continued publication of information concerning legislation, judicial practice, legal education and research in China. The yearbook was created in 1987.

76. Zhu Jingwen, 'Legal Profession in China: Achievement, Issues and Rethinking from the Perspective of Data Analysis' [2013] Social Sciences in Chinese Higher Education Institutions 117, 128.

77. Zhu (n 29) 105.

love or under which situations they can break up. In my view, it could be more suitable for morality to govern such a type of interpersonal relationship. People's mediation could be an appropriate mechanism in this sense. A boy, however deep his love for his girlfriend is, cannot request a judgment from a court requiring his girlfriend to restore the relationship with him. Unlike contractual parties who can void the contract under certain situations, a boy cannot request the court to revoke his girlfriend's decision to break up with him. However, the rift between these lovers can possibly be healed through people's mediation. As a third party, a mediator (e.g., a kind woman or an aged man) is likely to facilitate the communication between these two angry, disappointed, or silent lovers. The mediator can utilize flexible working methods such as getting to know the true feelings of the lovers and help them clarify the misunderstandings. This hypothetical case shows how people's mediation can solve conflicts in household affairs or interpersonal relationship and fill the gaps left by litigation. It is not to say that people's mediation will definitely and successfully resolve such disputes. Instead, it offers another option for disputants.

4.4.3   An Important Link of Big Mediation

Both people's mediation and adjudication are a part of the network of Big Mediation, which is lead by the China Communist Party. Cohen summarizes that: "A cardinal principle of this system was that the local group generally required the parties to exhaust their remedies within the group before looking to the magistrate for relief."[78] A similar situation still exists today, but there are a few changes. The parties are permitted to bring the issues before a court if they are not satisfied with the mediation results.

To fill the gaps between judicial systems and non-judicial systems, the Supreme People's Court unites the efforts of people's courts, administrative organs, social organizations, enterprises, and public institutions. It aims to build a communication and cooperation mechanism between adjudication and arbitration, administrative mediation, people's mediation, commercial mediation, and other non-judicial ways of solving disputes.[79] People's mediation is not considered as the sole means to tackle all types of disputes. Where the mediation fails to solve disputes, the parties concerned are still free to resort to arbitration, administrative mediation, or adjudication for resolutions. Thus, under Article 26 of People's Mediation Act, when mediation does not work, mediators shall terminate the mediation process and notify the parties concerned that they may protect their interests through arbitration, administrative means or judicial means. That is to say, people's mediation cannot prevent parties from turning to other dispute-solving approaches.

---

78. Cohen (n 73) 1223.
79. Supreme People's Court (n 74).

4.4.4   *Judicial Recognition and Enforcement of Mediation Agreements*

Where mediation is successfully held, a corresponding written mediation agreement can be made by people's mediators. When the parties agree not to conclude a written mediation agreement, an oral one can be made; however, the mediators shall note the contents of the oral agreement. A written mediation agreement may cover the following aspects: the parties' basic personal information; major facts of the dispute and the liabilities of all parties concerned; the provisions of the mediation agreement; and the way and term of fulfilling the agreement.

A mediation agreement is a civil contract in essence, and the agreement regulates civil rights and obligations.[80] Since people's mediation is a non-judicial way of solving civil disputes, the fulfillment of corresponding mediation agreements depends on party autonomy. Similar to a breach of contract or contract disputes, the parties concerned may refuse to perform a mediation agreement, or the parties may have different understandings of the provisions of a mediation agreement. In these situations, they could file a lawsuit for possible remedies.

In practice, the parties may either request for a judicial recognition of the legal effect or judicial enforcement of the agreement. The parties concerned may jointly apply to the people's court for judicial confirmation within 30 days after the mediation becomes effective, which makes it possible for the parties to request judicial enforcement when the mediation agreement was not performed. And if a people's court confirms that the mediation agreement is invalid, the parties concerned may either alter the original agreement or reach a new agreement through people's mediation. They may also lodge a lawsuit directly.[81]

The People's Mediation Act does not provide substantial criteria for when courts can decide whether or not to grant judicial recognition of a mediation agreement. However, due to the nature of a mediation agreement (a contract), courts make their decision based on the validity of such an agreement. Specifically speaking, courts will void an agreement if it: (i) damages the interests of the State; (ii) violates compulsory provisions of laws and administrative regulations; (iii) damages third parties' interests; (iv) infringes social ethics; or (v) was reached because parties were compelled bymediators.[82] Besides, parties can apply for withdrawing the recognition of an

---

80. Ibid.
81. See Article 33 of the People's Mediation Act.
82. See Article 7 of Several Provisions of the Supreme People's Court on the Judicial Confirmation Procedure for the People's Mediation Agreements (2011).

agreement under certain cases.[83] After the judicial confirmation, parties can ask a court to enforce the agreement.[84]

To summarize, people's mediation is a supplement rather than an alternative to adjudication. Firstly, these two approaches have their own features, which decide their diverging scope of application in resolving disputes. Although their material scope is overlapping, there are gaps left by adjudication. Secondly, the establishment and reform of the people's mediation system is not to replace judicial system. On the contrary, it aims to provide another channel of remedy for disputants, enhancing their confidence in realizing justice. For instance, people's mediation is more flexible in procedures than adjudication, which might be welcomed by particular people. In addition, the background of the increased position of private actors is that local courts suffer from caseload and public distrust. Thirdly, people's mediation committees and courts have different natures – the former are nongovernmental organizations, and the latter are national judicial organs. In parallel with this, the success of people's mediation depends on the parties' voluntary enforcement of mediation compromise or agreement. When one of the parties regrets and refuses to enforce these agreements, the other side can only resort to a court for adjudication. In other words, adjudication has the final say on the resolution of conflicts. However, the adjudication alone cannot sufficiently satisfy the needs of parties in this diversified stranger society. Their coexistence can promote the establishment of a multilevel dispute resolution system.

4.5   THE FUTURE IMPROVEMENT OF PEOPLE'S MEDIATION

Mediation is often criticized because it cannot provide disputants with similar remedies as litigation can; worse still, mediation may not comply with the rule of law.[85] People's mediation is also faced with such challenges. Minzner views the preference of mediation in judicial practice as a phenomenon of "turning against law".[86] The procedural deficiency of people's mediation also prompts doubts. Huang states that the sole emphasis on mediation results can serve to "excuse or cover up gross injustices" rather than uphold justice.[87] Another doubt concerns the leadership of the China Communist Party in the Big Mediation network. Mcguire comments that China endorses "rule by law" rather than the "rule of law". The "rule by law" respects

---

83. See Article 6 of Some Provisions of the Supreme People's Court on Trying Civil Cases Involving the People's Conciliation Agreements (2002).
84. See Article 33 of the People's Mediation Act.
85. Albert H. Y. Chen, 'Mediation, Litigation, and Justice – Confucian Reflections in A Modern Liberal Society', in Daniel A. Bell and Hahm Chaibong (eds), *Confucianism for the Modern World* (Cambridge University Press 2003) 259-271.
86. Minzner (n 11) 935-984.
87. Huang (n 71) 68.

the values of laws in regulating society, but it does not recognize laws as "the supreme authority" to social management. It is 'the Party' rather than 'the court' that has the final authority.[88] In the CPC plenary meeting of 2014, the ties between the Party's leadership and rule of law are illustrated – the CPC is the leader of rule of law in China. The CPC declares that "Party's leadership is the most essential feature of the socialism with Chinese characteristics, and the most fundamental guarantee of socialist rule of law". Moreover, it reaffirms that the party's leadership and the rule of law is consistent with each other – 'socialist rule of law must adhere to the Party's leadership, while the Party's leadership must rely on socialist rule of law'.[89]

In this context, this section analyzes the problems in practice and makes comments on the future development of people's mediation. Firstly, the relationship among people's mediation committees, government (or the Party), and courts should be further clarified. Under the Big Mediation network, it may be difficult for people's mediation to be neutral. On the other hand, parties could be under more pressure because they have to resolve disputes with such a big interference from the network. As indicated above, the network is led by the China Communist Party and involves judicial organs (e.g., courts), administrative organs (local governments), and non-judicial organs (e.g., people's mediation committees). As a non-governmental organization, a people's mediation may play a weak role and function in the mediation process.

Pursuant to the People's Mediation Act, people's mediation committees must accept governments and courts' instructions.[90] Governments' instructions concern: (i) adopting relevant policies and regulations about the aims and working plan of local mediation committees; (ii) assisting or participating in mediation upon the request of people's mediation committees or practical needs, especially when there are hard cases; (iii) reviewing people's mediation agreements and requiring people's mediation committees to notice parties when the agreement infringes law, state policies or public orders; and (iv) training people's mediators. Local courts also help to train mediators through lecturing legal knowledge and mediation skills. Courts can communicate their opinions about issues in people's mediation and relevant proposals to both governments and people's mediation committees.[91] As could be seen from the description above, governments and courts could have a great influence or even interference on people's mediation. This may undermine the independence and impartiality of people's mediation.

---

88. James E. Mcguire, 'Rule of Law and ADR in China – Observations on Recent Developments' [2010] Dispute Resolution Magazine 20.
89. See 'CPC Central Committee's Decision on Major Issues concerning Comprehensively Advancing Rule of Law' and 'An explanation on the CPC Central Committee's Decision on Major Issues concerning Comprehensively Advancing Rule of Law'.
90. See Article 5 of People's Mediation Act.
91. Wang, Hao (n 18) 19-23.

Secondly, people's mediation is faced with challenges to ensure party autonomy. This is because social and judicial pressure can negatively affect individuals' will in whether accepting a mediation result or not. Such pressure can be generated by many factors. On the one hand, the disputants often have different bargaining power in the mediation process. Those who have weaker bargaining power may be forced to agree to mediation results.[92] Thus the mediation agreement may not reflect the true will of weaker parties. On the other hand, mediators are likely to present the 'public opinion of the community'. Therefore, the mediation may not pay enough attention to the position of the disputants but local customs.[93] Thirdly, the people's mediation system does not take measures to ensure that such weaker parties realize justice based on an equal negotiation. Mediators who are familiars of disputants may determine who is right or wrong according to his prior assessment of behavior of both disputants rather than based on the facts and law. Such possible prejudice of mediators could also undermine individuals' will to resort to people's mediation.[94] Fourthly, the Supreme People's Court makes people's mediation a suggested first step in the process of dispute resolution, and local courts make extrajudicial mediation a suggested (in some cases even compulsory) pretrial step. In practice, many local courts establish the so-called a 'window of people's mediation' – a procedure that guides parties to solve disputes through people's mediation before trial.[95] This procedure has no binding force and is targeted to normal and simple disputes. Nevertheless, this prompts the question of protecting individuals' litigation rights and party autonomy in choosing their preferred way to solve conflicts. In summary, the People's Mediation Act recognizes the importance of disputes' individual will in mediation, but there lacks such a mechanism that ensure mediation will be carried out in accordance with law.

Thirdly, both the procedure of people's mediation and the draft of people's mediation agreements should be improved. People's mediation has an advantage of utilizing flexible mediation procedure, but this could also generate side effects. There are three types of disadvantages.[96] Firstly, the mediation procedure lacks standardization. For example, there are no records of investigation of mediation in some cases. This may cause difficulties of proving the contents of agreements when the parties hold different understandings concerning mediation results. Secondly, due to the lack of legal

---

92. Huang (n 71) 68-204. Chen (n 85).

93. Fei (n 26) 61-62.

94. James and Michael demonstrated that "To the Chinese mediators, knowledge of the disputants is a major asset that enables them to determine who is right or wrong in a dispute." They continued to detail some examples drawn from their interviews: "I know him. He is the worst miser I have ever seen"; "She is a lazy wife"; or "He is my cousin. I can believe him." See Wall, Blum (n 2) 8-9.

95. See Article 8 of the Notice of the Supreme People's Court on Issuing Several Opinions on Further Implementing the Work Principle of 'Giving Priority to Mediation and Combining Mediation with Judgment' (*Guanyu Jinyibu Guanche Tiaojie Youxian Tiaopan Jiehe Gongzuo Yuanze De Ruogan Yijian*), No. 16 in 2010.

96. Zhejiang Higher People's Court, 'The Investigation on Judicial Confirmation of People's Mediation Agreements (*Guanyu Renmin Tiaojie Xieyi Sifa Queren De Diaoyan*)' [2010] People's Judicature 63, 64-66.

knowledge, some mediators may cause the parties to make an agreement that is not in accordance with law. Thirdly, the draft of mediation agreements may be of low quality. For instance, there are conflicts in phrase or the names of parties are not listed completely. Last but not least, although People's Mediation Act expressly allows disputants to apply for judicial recognition of people's mediation agreement, it does not stipulate the remedies and procedures for wrong judicial confirmation. If such a judicial recognition damages third parties' interests, should the third parties be entitled to lodge an appeal or just to request the court of first instance to withdraw the confirmation? The statute does not provide an answer. Similar questions as this raise many debates in judicial practice, so the Supreme People's Court should enact more specific procedures and rules.

As could be seen from the above-mentioned three problematic aspects of people's mediation, there is desire for bringing people's mediation right on track – the rule of law. China government's preference of mediation or big mediation should not undermine the authority of litigation. Measures should be taken to ensure the independence and impartiality of mediation, to normalize mediation procedure and document making, and to protect party autonomy.

4.6   Conclusion

China embarks on seeking an appropriate approach, which could ensure social harmony and stability, to the resolution of social disputes. People's mediation gradually becomes a suggested channel for resolving disputes in this context. As an oriental experience, people's mediation is characterized by its extrajudicial nature and flexibility of procedures. The People's Mediation Act lays the foundation for the regime of people's mediation. Its position and structures of organization has been changed. This article mainly described latest changes of people's mediation and mediation committees, analyzed the legitimacy of such changes, pinpointed the relationship between people's mediation and litigation and underlined problematic aspects of people's meditation and relevant future improvements.

One of the striking developments of people's mediation is the increased position of private actors in mediation process. Retired judges, academics, lawyers, and other individuals are welcomed by people's mediation. Besides, many professional or specialized mediation organizations have been established in hospitals, stock markets and other fields. Under the mechanism of the Big Mediation, governments, people's mediation committees, courts, and other parties work together on resolving disputes. These changes could be explained from cultural, political, and social perspectives. Confucianism, especially the ideal of harmony, continues to have an influence on both Party policies and judicial reform. Since

China is in the transitional period, new types of cases frequently emerge, which deepens the desire to launch diversified mechanisms of dispute resolution. People's mediation becomes a part of such a multi-layered regime and sticks to party autonomy.

Nevertheless, the promotion of people's mediation does not deny the function of litigation, for people's mediation is a supplementary rather than an alternative to adjudication. China judicial practice places more weight on social effects generated by adjudication, which facilitates the connection between litigation process and people's mediation. Under the Big Mediation network, people's mediation and litigation coexist with each other. People's mediation can fill the gaps left by litigation, while people's mediation agreements need courts' confirmation. In spite of such mutual beneficial cooperation, there are conflicts between people's mediation and litigation. The relationship among people's mediation committees, government (or the Party), and courts should be further clarified; otherwise, the independence and impartiality of people's mediation would be undermined. Social and judicial pressure can have a negative influence on individuals' willing to accept a mediation result or not, but measures to protect party autonomy are lacking. What is worse, the procedure of people's mediation and the draft of people's mediation agreements have defects. These phenomena raise the doubt of turning against law. The future development of people's mediation depends on how China responses to such challenges and brings people's mediation on the track. China should ensure the independence and impartiality of people's mediation, normalize mediation procedure and document making, and protect party autonomy.

Previously Published in the Governance & Recht Series